MORE GIVE TO LIVE

MORE
GIVE TO
LIVE HOW
GIVING
CAN
CHANGE
YOUR
LIFE

Douglas M. Lawson, Ph.D.

ALTI
PUBLISHING

Library of Congress Catalog Card number 91-041165

ISBN 1-883051-22-3

Printed in the United States of America

10 9 8 7 6 5 4 3 2 1

For information or additional copies, contact:
        ALTI Publishing
        P.O. Box 16
        La Jolla, CA 92038
        Tel: (858) 452-7703
        FAX: (858) 452-7702
        Email: sorourke@alticorp.com

Quantity Discounts Available

If you want happiness
for an hour — take a nap.
If you want happiness
for a day — go fishing.
If you want happiness
for a month — get married.
If you want happiness
for a year — inherit a fortune.
If you want happiness
for a lifetime — help someone else.

CHINESE PROVERB

CONTENTS

ACKNOWLEDGMENTS

Books like *Give to Live* and *More Give to Live* are the direct result of a gift to me of the writing and editing talents of many dedicated people. I want to single out for a special word of gratitude the assistance of the late Dan Fitzgibbon and Adam McCoy. Without Dan's ability to translate my spoken words into readable prose and Adam's talent for organizing and rewriting, this book would not have been possible.

I also want to thank Cynthia Glacken for introducing me to Dan and to Renni Browne. Renni, Adam, and others with her remarkable company, The Editorial Department — notably Jane Rafal and Dave King — brought a great deal of professionalism and hard work to *Give to Live*. Without the excellent, time-consuming work of Janet Dick and Theresa Alexander the final manuscript of *More Give to Live* never would have been completed.

More Give to Live has been a part of my presentations at seminars and lectures for years. My debt of gratitude to the many participants who have shared their observations on giving is beyond calculation. As for my professional colleagues, friends, and clients through the years who have helped me, I truly wish I had the space to list their names. But to several I owe a special word of thanks: Art Frantzreb, Dr. Robert Schuller, Dr. John Haggai, Millard and Linda Fuller, Jerry Panas, Milton Murray, Chancellor John Montford, Dr. James Daughdrill and Ann Grimm, who gave me the original book's title.

Barbara Taylor deserves the credit for introducing me to Manuel Arango, founder and president of the Mexican Center for the Study of Philanthropy. It was he who took the mighty risk in arranging for ALTI Publishing to bring out this unknown author's work. To him and his faith in me, I owe a great deal. I also want to thank Wayne Hilbig, President of ALTI, for his encouragement and support of *More Give to Live* in its many incarnations.

Beyond these special people who encouraged me in the writing of this book, I would like to acknowledge the example of true giving my mother and father set for me as a child. This book really started with the spirit they shared with me.

And finally, I want the world to know that without the unconditional gift of love to me every day on the part of a white, eight-pound Maltese dog named Popcorn, I might never have persevered.

FOREWORD

Dr. Robert H. Schuller

Doug Lawson has been a colleague and friend of mine for more than twenty-two years. I met him in 1976 on Maundy Thursday, as we set out to begin raising the $20 million needed to build the Crystal Cathedral.

Our first professional visit together was to John Crean, founder and retired chairman of Fleetwood Enterprises, a Fortune 500 company based in Riverside, California. Mr. Crean called me the next day, Good Friday, to say he would be happy to be the first $1 million giver to the Crystal Cathedral.

Doug Lawson is largely responsible for our having raised the balance of the money for this magnificent building. He is still a consultant to our ministry, his wise counsel valued by us all. Early in our relationship he taught me his philosophy of the joy of giving, and it has been etched on my mind and ministry ever since.

An ordained United Methodist minister, Dr. Lawson began his ministry at the age of eighteen by building a Methodist church in Hampton, Virginia. He went on to earn a Ph.D. from Duke University in religion and history, but it was at that little church in Hampton that Doug began to develop his philosophy of giving. That philosophy has been the key to a remarkable career in which he has raised literally hundreds of millions of dollars for worthy causes and charities in America and all over the world.

Dr. Lawson is one of the most important figures in the extraordinary American world of generous giving, and in these pages he shares with readers his years of experience. We have plenty of books on fundraising but very few on giving, and none that tell us how giving benefits the giver. *More Give to Live* is a pioneering book that is badly needed by all of us as individuals and as a society.

In *More Give to Live*, Doug shows how scientists are coming around to one of the most important lessons I have learned in all my years in the ministry. People come to life —become fully alive, aware, and joyful — when they help others. It is one of the great teachings of the Christian, Jewish, and Muslim religions that God loves us when we love each other, when we share His love with other human beings.

Jesus says, "It is better to give than to receive." And St. Paul says, "God loves a cheerful giver." New researchers agree: giving is the key to abundant life. When we share with others, we are sharing the love of God with them. And the great secret of God's love is that the more we share it, the more of it there is to share.

More Give to Live tells the inspiring and exciting story of what happens to us when we give. We deepen and enrich our own lives to an extraordinary degree as we give to others. Giving helps us share in God's work of creation. When we link ourselves to each other through volunteer work and charitable giving, we are linking ourselves to the love of God.

The effect of giving, sharing, volunteering, and working for a better world is both wonderfully simple and wonderfully practical. We have better lives. And as Doug Lawson makes so clear, our lives are made better in every possible way — physically, psychologically, and emotionally as well as morally.

This is a great story. I hope you read Doug's book with care and put its wisdom into practice. Your life will be better, and so will the world.

INTRODUCTION

Many of us give up our lives by the time we reach twenty-one. We don't go to an early grave, thanks to medical science, but far too many of us lose our life force, our direction, and our purpose. The challenge is age-old: how are we to live and enjoy our lives fully? The threefold approach set forth in this book is one practical solution to that dilemma.

First, we need a *purpose* fit to live for. Second, we need to become comfortable with and accept who we are — we need to be *selves* fit to live with. Finally, we need a *faith* fit to live by.

So how do we find this meaning? How do we develop a self that we can be comfortable with? Most importantly, just where do we find faith that can empower and enrich others and us? Our library shelves are filled with popular psychology books, quick-fix menus, and obscure rituals that promise heaven on earth, a magic land of plenty, a quiet place where we can hear our heart sing. Of those few books that make good on these promises, most are simply ancient material dressed up in contemporary clothes. Their theories rarely break new ground and even more rarely offer measurable evidence to back up the theories.

More Give to Live, a completely revised and enlarged edition of the original *Give to Live,* does not promise more than it can deliver, nor does it present itself as the only solution to the troubles that beset us. What it does do is offer you a new way of looking at your life. This angle of approach arises out of startling new information about the measurable, proven benefits you can gain from giving. These benefits include longer life, a lower level of stress, a stronger immune system, a stronger heart — literally as well as figuratively. The book outlines a program, a series of steps anyone can take that can lead you to greater emotional well-being, an enhanced ability to cope with daily problems, and a heightened appreciation of your own life.

In this book you will learn what some of the most honored medical doctors, psychotherapists, and scientists of our age have to say about the benefits of extending yourself to benefit others. Now we have new evidence that shows how we can help heal ourselves when we reach out to help others.

More Give to Live looks at the entire philanthropic process: the extent of giving (we are a phenomenally, uniquely generous nation); what motivates us to give; and what sabotages our efforts and deprives us of much of the richness of the experience. It lays out effective steps you can take to get involved, increase your ability to make a real difference in the world, and enjoy the philanthropic journey.

More Give to Live holds forth a bold promise: If you want more out of your life and are willing to take some simple steps along the "giving path," you can have a richer, fuller, happier existence. I invite you to try the program of action set forth in these pages. I invite you to believe me when I say that you have everything to gain and absolutely nothing to lose from a life of giving.

O•N•E

A TROUBLED
BUT GIVING NATION

A Search for Meaning

Deeds of giving are the very foundation of the world.
THE TORAH

All is not well in Camelot. Millions of Americans are profoundly unhappy with their lives. Many are isolated, unconnected, adrift, lost. Family ties are tenuous. Divorce, disease, and debt race like plagues through city and suburb. Tension, aggression, and the scramble to survive take a terrible toll. Marital setbacks, loneliness, and despair seem to form an endless river threatening to submerge us. Hostility, crime, and alienation seem to outpace progress.

Our problems are legion, and many of us feel increasingly helpless as our control slips and stress mounts. Economic hardship and declining income make guests of anxiety and apprehension in many homes that once seemed secure. Untold numbers of Americans suffer and yet persevere. If you listen carefully, you can hear the urgency in their voices when they describe what they want: freedom from illness, financial security, safety, happiness, contentment, peace of mind. Above all they want some measure of control over our increasingly bewildering world. They want a secure, meaningful existence.

What we are experiencing is not new. In his first sermon, many centuries ago, the Buddha described much of what is now confronting us. To a small group of followers he set forth his beliefs. The first: that existence is full of conflict, dissatisfaction, sorrow, and suffering. The second: that suffering begins in our own selfish desires, craving for pleasure, and avoidance of pain. In short, we are the architects of our own difficulties.

Some two hundred years ago, the French educator Alexis de Tocqueville came to America to study our newly independent republic. In *Democracy in America* he points to elements of colonial life that still describe Americans today: "I have seen the freest and best-educated of men in circumstances the happiest to be found in the world. Yet it seemed to me that a cloud habitually hung on their brow and they seemed serious and almost sad in their pleasures. They never stop thinking of the good things they have not got. They clutch everything and hold nothing fast."

We have grown more knowledgeable and secure over the last two hundred years, but I suspect that our sadness has deepened, our envy has increased, and the furrowed brow has given way to a perpetual scowl. Our "pursuit of happiness" seems to lead us into more and more unsettling times.

What seems to pull us back from the brink of despair and disillusionment is our energy, our belief in good, our faith, and our dogged determination. The forces that hammer at us have turned us into a nation of seekers. Part of our search has been prompted by a sense that much of life is empty, confusing, monotonous, unrewarding. We search for meaning and inspiration, for a workable formula that can lead us to a joyful, contented, satisfying existence.

As a nation we seem almost to have forgotten how to enjoy life. We seem unable to take a minute and smell the spring flowers or gaze at a glowing sunset. When we lose joy we lose some of our freedom, some of our sense of community; and because we sense this loss, we try mightily to recapture it.

In our dissatisfaction many of us turn to religion, to enlightened teachers, gifted therapists, or charismatic leaders. In increasing numbers, we find strength and guidance in support groups and we devour self-help books and tapes. For most of us, the religious community has become the place where we can search for meaning and clarity.

Seven out of ten American adults now attend religious services; the influence of this religious guidance probably makes it the most positive force operating in America today. It nurtures and directs us, tempers discontent, quiets the hostile heart. The religious community at its best promotes solidarity, brotherly love, compassion, and acceptance. It supports us in moments of distress and pain and asks us to do the same for our neighbor.

Through the ages, people have tried to eliminate conflict and suffering, to experience lives of value and purpose. Many solutions have been advanced over many centuries. One that has endured calls on us to "do unto others as we would have them do unto us." This "golden" rule is the primary law of peaceful coexistence. Partly out of compassion and responsibility, partly for survival or self-protection, people support the institutions they cherish. Churches, synagogues, meetinghouses, and mosques act as counterbalances to the acquisitive, self-centered, aggressive spirit that undermines so much of our higher purpose. The cult of rugged individualism — man alone against the world — is challenged by many institutions but especially by the religious community. The truth is, we cannot survive and find enjoyment through isolation and personal power. A successful life, full of meaning, calls for close cooperation, respect for the rights of others, and compassion.

The Golden Rule in still the best path to a rewarding and healthy life. As Dr. William Redford puts it in his book *The Trusting Heart,* "The core of Christianity and all the other major religions is that we should treat others as we would like them to treat us."

Since you are reading this book, you are likely to be looking for meaning, a better reason for living — and a better way of living. In your search, you might give some thought to these questions:

- How satisfied are you with the way your life is going?
- What personal problems and issues bother you most?
- Are you really happy with your present state of health?
- Is there room in your life for more giving, and if so, what's holding you back?
- Would you like to have more attention, affection, and love in your life?
- Do you believe that giving and sharing who you are (and what you have) could make you measurably happier and healthier?
- How much of your life is "on hold," waiting for something to happen?

Think about your responses and where you are in your life. Then read on. Hopefully you will find some solutions in the following pages.

A Caring Spirit

Love is not getting but giving.
Marie Dressler

Despite all our tension, discontent, and the rampaging forces of acquisitiveness, America is the most giving and caring nation on the face of the earth. Our generosity and benevolence surpass that of all other nations — apparently our well-publicized troubles have not blunted our compassion and concern for others. During my forty-four years of work with nonprofit organizations, (thirty-two of them as a professional fundraiser), I have watched annual philanthropic giving grow from $15 billion to $143.5 billion.

Through lean and prosperous years alike, Americans have customarily given more to charity than they did the previous year. Boom or bust, we as a nation care more than ever about the welfare — health, education, recreation and spirituality — of others. Two hundred years ago, de Tocqueville singled out our forefathers' commitment to help, house, and nurture less fortunate neighbors. He wrote with amazement about our sense of community and charitable actions, about the way these values strengthened us as a new society. And the words de Tocqueville wrote back then are still true today.

Since the birth of our republic, giving, sharing and volunteering have brought us together and given many of us a sense of purpose. Americans have consistently shown compassion for others along with a passion for freedom.

I believe benevolence to be a powerful force that has contributed to our success as a nation and our concern for others (despite our own problems) to be an expression of our highest ideals. I'm also convinced that the giving spirit has done much to bring together the diverse populations of our vast country. Our giving ways have become a palpable demonstration of our willingness to help our neighbors.

Caring and sharing in America take many forms, from local volunteer efforts to feed the homeless to the benevolence of families like the Annenbergs, who recently donated more than $300 million to the United Negro College Fund. Our donations are diverse and help preserve the wilderness as well as make it possible for parents to stay with their children during cancer treatment. The list of benevolent acts is almost endless: Where there is a need, there is almost always a concerned community group or institution ready to help.

When we see a need we often give our time, talent, and emotional energy along with our money. The sheer scale of our giving is staggering. In 1997, according to *Giving USA,* more than $143 billion was given to nonprofits in America. Corporations and foundations accounted for approximately 15 percent of all giving, but the greatest amount by far of that incredible sum was given by individuals (76.2 percent). Giving by individuals increased by 6.8 percent in 1991 and by nearly 7 percent in 1996.

SOURCE	PERCENT OF TOTAL $ DONATED
Individuals	76.2
Bequests	8.8
Foundations	9.3
Corporations	5.7

However statistics do not really capture the spirit, personal involvement, and concern that attend these gifts.

When raging floodwaters devastated the low-lying areas of the north central United States in 1997 — sweeping away communities, destroying homes, and leaving thousands homeless — the entire nation responded. Individuals and corporations gave money, talent, and labor to help the victims. If you travel through that area today, you will find new homes standing where old ones were destroyed. Many of these were rebuilt with money donated to nonprofit organizations like Habitat for Humanity, one of whose volunteer workers is former president Jimmy Carter.

Some people contributed "gifts in kind," such as art, real estate, food, and clothing. Others, like Joan Kroc, the widow of the founder of McDonalds', arranged to help each and every soggy household in Rapid City with $2,500 in cash to help them dig out, repair, or start rebuilding. Her efforts to remain anonymous were to no avail, for the media were relentless in their paper chase to find such a kind donor.

Rock stars donate their time and talents to raise money for financially failing farmers, AIDS victims, and the homeless. A movie star, Celeste Holm, charges fifty cents for her autograph and gives the money to a famine-relief organization. Paul Newman gives all the profits from the food products bearing his name to charity, $67 million to date. Garrison Keillor gave the profits from his best-selling book to public radio. These are just a few of the ways in which people from all walks of life express their concern and compassion.

A wonderful example of sharing from the American past is a traditional "barn raising." In early rural America a barn was essential, and a farmer whose barn burned down was in deep trouble. If a storm, fire, or flood destroyed the barn, the whole community immediately banded together to raise a new one. It mattered little that the stricken farmer was of a different faith or from a different homeland or even a virtual stranger. He was in trouble, his neighbors cared, and their care and concern bonded them together.

Barn raisings may have largely disappeared from the American scene, but the spirit lives on. While economic conditions and lifestyles are very different today, the compassion and caring that nourished early America are still evident in the fabric of everyday American life. Institutions have changed and problems have become more complex, but the response is largely the same. The affluent help the impoverished, those who can read teach the illiterate, corporations support communities, the elderly are protected and aided by the young. And those who serve a loving God out of faith nurture the spirit of their religion. There is a richness in the fabric of American life, rooted in giving and volunteering. It is present in good times and in bad.

In Houston, Texas, during the sharp decline in oil prices in the mid-1980s, individuals and corporations alike were going bankrupt faster than new jobs could be created. The numbers of homeless swelled as whole families joined the ranks of the desperate and destitute. The corporate leaders and charitable foundations of Houston, along with concerned citizens like George Bush, reached into their overworked pockets to build one of the finest homeless shelters for women and children in America. It was my privilege to be a part of that fundraising campaign, and if you visit the Star of Hope Family Shelter you will see not just a well-constructed haven, but also a tribute to America's giving spirit.

The table below from *Giving USA* shows who were the beneficiaries of the funds donated in 1996 by Americans.

WHO BENEFITS FROM GIVING	PERCENT IN 1996, TOTAL $ GIVEN
Religion	46.1
Human services	8.1
Education	12.5
Health	9.2
Arts/culture/humanities	7.2
Public/society benefit	5.0
Other organizations	11.9

Americans traditionally give a major portion of their charitable money to religious organizations. In 1996 religious gifts dipped slightly over the previous year, while contributions to education showed modest gains.

The Independent Sector reported some positive facts about American giving in a 1996 study entitled "Giving and Volunteering in the United States":

- Almost seven out of ten U.S. households contributed to charitable organizations in 1996.

- The average household contribution was $1,017 annually, about 2.2 percent of total family income. Some ninety-five million households gave money to charities.

- Total households contributing slipped slightly from 73 percent to 69 percent in 1996. However, the actual dollars given were up $889 million.

- Giving is as concentrated as personal wealth. Just as a large proportion of the nation's wealth is concentrated in the hands of a fortunate few, only 20 percent of all U.S. households accounted for 70 percent of all contributions.

- The poor appear to be more compassionate than the wealthy. Moderate- and low-income Americans contributed proportionately more of their income to charity. Families earning less than $10,000 annually donated an impressive 4.3 percent of their yearly income.

- Age also strongly influences contributions. Contributors in the twenty-five to thirty-four age bracket gave only 1.6 percent of their annual income, while those fifty-five to seventy-four gave twice as much (3.4 percent).

How does one classify the philanthropic actions of an elderly African-American and domestic who labored all her life on a very limited income but donated all of her life savings ($150,000) to a local college even though she herself had very little formal education? Despite her humble request for anonymity, Oseola McCarthy's identity was revealed and she became a celebrity and national "power of example," appearing on *Oprah* and numerous other nationwide and worldwide television talk shows. On the day the first scholarship was announced, the young African-American recipient said she would accept it only on one condition — that Oseola McCarthy be present at her graduation. When the eighty-four-year-old donor said, that she would be there, the audience burst into applause. What a reason to keep on living! I have never heard of a better one.

It's inspiring to wade through the Independent Sector statistics and uncover such reassuring finds as these:

- Of those people seventy-five and older, 22 percent report that they only "had enough income to cover their basic necessities, yet they gave 2.2 percent of their meager income ($267 on average) to charity.

- Oddly enough, about one-fourth of all U.S. contributors have no clear idea how their giving compares to that of others like themselves, but their typical annual contribution is just under $1,000 (about average for all contributors).

- One of the most important factors influencing how much a person gives is their attendance at religious services. Those who regularly attend services accounted for a whopping 80 percent of all giving (2.3 percent of their incomes). Those who don't attend services gave only 1.1 percent of their incomes annually.

A religious or spiritual connection is clearly a major driving force behind much of America's benevolence. It is also a major impetus to volunteering. People who attend religious services weekly are the most likely to volunteer. According to Virginia Hodgkinson, formerly of Independent Sector, "The schools stopped teaching moral values a long time ago. Mom's working, so there's not as much guidance at home. Parents are turning to churches for help." Newsweek reported that children are leading their parents back to churches and synagogues, and as Virginia Hodgkinson and Robert Wuthnow point out in their book Faith and Philanthropy in America, the linkage between religion and giving in America remains solid.

It is heartening to see that charitable contributions in America continue to outpace inflation and economic growth. The bad news is that our need for more services grows greater with each passing year. America is a giving nation at heart, and it is this caring spirit that forms the foundation upon which this nation is built.

Philanthropy Is People-to-People

Our work brings people face-to-face with love.
To us what matters is an individual.
To get to love the person we must have
close contact with him.

MOTHER TERESA

Some people express their compassion and concern by donating in response to an "arm's-length" solicitation, an appeal letter, or a telethon with an 800 number, but for most people the essence of giving is found in some form of direct contact. Personal involvement is most rewarding, whether it involves providing food for the homeless, organizing a church or college program to benefit blind children, or pitching in to clean up a community after a flood. No matter how intensely the media depicts the need for monetary contributions, personal contact still adds an extra dimension.

Hands-on involvement, volunteer effort, and personal dedication are what provide the most benefit to both the recipient or recipient organization and the volunteer. The miracle of people-to-people involvement lies in seeing one's mission — reaching the needy people — and making a real difference by your presence and guidance. Consider some further findings from the 1996 Independent Sector study about how we are involved:

- About 49 percent of all adult Americans claimed that they undertook some kind of organized volunteer work, donating an average of 4.2 hours per week.
- Much of this volunteer effort was formal (scheduled work within an organization). The combined efforts

of these millions of adults produced a monumental annual total of twenty billion volunteer hours — which is the equivalent of the efforts of nine million full-time employees. The dollar value of this volunteer effort is estimated to be $201 billion yearly — a sum that surpasses the total dollars given in 1996.

- Leaving aside fundraising efforts, the most active areas of personal involvement consisted of donating time and talents:

PERSONALLY GAVE TIME TO:	PERCENT OF VOLUNTEERS:
Religious organizations	52
Educational institutions	30
Youth Development	28
Human Services	24
Health organizations	25
Recreation, sports activities	13

Not surprisingly, the typical volunteer reported giving time to at least two different organizations in the past year.

- There is a strong linkage between volunteering and giving. Those who both contributed money and volunteered gave an average of $1,203 to charity. Those who did not volunteer contributed an average of $268 in 1996.

- Only about one-third of people who were not members of a religious organization volunteered, but more than 60 percent of members of religious organizations volunteered.

- People offer many reasons for volunteering. Some talk about carrying on traditions that have long guided their families. Others participate because they are asked by relatives, friends, members of their

community, or people who represent a cause with
which they identify. Still others become involved
because they believe their efforts will benefit friends
or relatives.

- While millions of people give billions of hours in volunteer activities, only one in five of us "seek out" the
activity or assignment on our own. New volunteers
are more apt to be reactive than active; they wait to be
asked or assigned.

- Most people who become involved want to do something useful and meaningful. Almost two-thirds gave
this response when asked why they first volunteered.
(Source: 1988 Independent Sector report conducted
by the Gallup Organization.)

The patterns of philanthropy are shifting. People are
becoming involved in a greater variety of causes (there are
an estimated 600,000 active charitable or nonprofit organizations in the U.S.), and they are more concerned than
ever before about how effective their mission is. They also
want to be more involved in the organization's actual work
and to observe what is done with their contribution, which
means better accountability and clarity of purpose.

Today's contributors are more likely to want to experience their beliefs in action. The stronger the conviction,
the greater the personal involvement; the more direct the
contact, the larger the contribution or pledge. Although
they may find it difficult to verbalize their feelings about
why they volunteer, they clearly want to see or know that
their actions or donations make a difference. They gain
something special from being needed and appreciated and
from extending themselves and their resources. Many
speak of a spiritual satisfaction, an affirmation of what they

hold dear. All of these experiences are more likely to be found in volunteer activities where there is one-to-one contact, personal service, or expert guidance.

Volunteers tell me how giving has enriched their lives, enhanced their sense of self, and given special meaning to a stress-ridden existence. Recent studies by *Psychology Today, American Health,* and the Institute for Advancement of Health have referred to a "helper's high," a phrase first coined by Allan Luks. Social scientists and medical doctors are beginning to see how the human mind triggers special chemicals that enable volunteers to feel more expansive, even euphoric; these chemicals called endorphins are released during esteem-building activities such as working to help others. The Harvard cardiologist and author Dr. Herbert Benson states that altruistic acts can produce a relaxation response equivalent to a deep state of rest.

To many who give, it's the emotional benefits that lead them to volunteer. For others, it's a belief that added blessings will be showered on those who help. For still others it is a simple recognition that we are our brothers' keepers. To millions, volunteering represents what is right with the world: an act of philanthropy is an act of love. In a world filled with violence, hatred, and suspicion, giving is an expression of faith, trust, and concern. Giving is spiritually uplifting — a powerful testimony to our fundamental goodness. In my book *Volunteering: 101 Ways You Can Improve The World and Your Life,* I document this by answering the key questions volunteers often ask.

Much of this book is inspired by the emerging body of knowledge about the many benefits that attend acts of giving and sharing. Over the past decade, some forward-thinking social scientists and medical experts have quantified the relationship between philanthropic activities and the superior physical and emotional well-being that comes to people who engage in them.

While most people probably subscribe to the general theory that charity is "good for the soul," almost all would be hard-pressed to say why. Many would also be surprised to learn that philanthropic acts are also good for the mind and body. Research is now confirming these claims. These findings can help transform the way people live and feel about themselves. For years I have been one of a small group of people trying to show that philanthropy is a powerful emotional catalyst and safeguard of physical health, significantly more important to the well-being of mankind than was ever considered possible. Thoughtful people have begun to speak openly about the life-sustaining emotional, physical, and spiritual benefits generated by active giving. The results of these (now) large-scale inquiries confirm that philanthropic involvement is *measurably* wholesome to mind, body, and spirit.

Could it be that one solution to America's many troubles can be found in its caring spirit? The thesis of this book underscores the answer: a resounding Yes! Giving can change America. Giving can also change and improve your life — and the lives of everyone who inhabits the planet.

T·W·O

THE EXTRAORDINARY BENEFITS
OF GIVING

Living Longer and Living Healthier

There is a wonderful mythical law of nature that the three things we crave most in life, happiness, freedom, and peace *of mind, are always attained by giving them to someone else.*

Recent researchers who describe the extraordinary benefits that can come from giving include medical and social scientists such as Allan Luks, Arthur White, T. George Harris, Dr. Herbert Benson, Dr. David Sobel, Dr. Bernard Siegel, Dr. Sula Benet, Dr. Dean Ornish, and organizations like the Gallup Organization, *Prevention* magazine, the Roper Organization, and *American Health* magazine.

Until his death, Norman Cousins led a pioneering project at UCLA to study the issue of the mind's influence over the body. His last book, *Head First,* was a dramatic confirmation of a line from Shakespeare: "'Tis the mind that makes the body rich." Much of what Cousins discovered underlined the importance and value of philanthropy.

Professor Mihaly Cikszentmihalyi of the University of Chicago has for many years conducted a detailed inquiry into the psychology of peak experiences. In his acclaimed work *Flow: The Psychology of Peak Experience,* he examines emotional factors necessary for people to experience the pleasurable, health-sustaining mental state he describes as "flow." His findings help clarify the benefits of philanthropic behavior.

These new studies tell us that assisting others through acts of charity or devotion to causes improves our physical health. Giving is not just a minor influence on good health but the key to physical and mental well-being. The studies show that for all ages (but particularly among the elderly), one way to escape or minimize premature physical and emotional deterioration is by staying active in the service of others.

For example, a ten-year study of the physical health and social activities of 2,700 men in Tecumseh, Michigan, found that those who did regular volunteer work had death rates two-and-one-half times lower than those who didn't. Those who serve others may be on a new path to longevity. Many noted philanthropists outlived most of their contemporaries — Ford, Rockefeller, Kroc, Mellon, Carnegie, McGaw, Packard, and Annenberg, to name just a few — and while their access to superior medical care undoubtedly helped them live longer, there is every reason to assume that their work and donations to others also extended their lives.

If you want to have a long, satisfying, and active life, you might wish to consider some unusual but important findings of Dr. Sula Benet, an anthropologist and professor at Hunter College, Columbia, and Harvard. Dr. Benet and her research crew spent five summers in the Russian Caucasus region, trying to determine just which human dynamics conspired to produce an incredible concentration of superannuated elders. In this area of the world can be found hundreds of mentally alert and physically active individuals who are in the second century of their life (more than one hundred years old). Soviet research records have authenticated the incredible claims that many of these hardy and rugged farmers and mountain folks live to be 140 to 150 years of age.

Dr. Benet's mission was to interview these truly "senior" citizens and hopefully discover the specific factors and activities that contribute significantly to an active and "ever-so-long" life span. As many of us know, life is truly precious and just who among us wouldn't like to extend a healthy and productive life well into the 120 to 150 age range, which is just about twice as long as the current U.S. mortality rate of 75 years.

In her painstaking research activities, Dr. Benet did manage to isolate and identify certain critical components that heavily contributed to longevity. It is heartening to note that caregiving and helping less-fortunate relatives and others is built into their basic response to life's challenges and calamities.

The primary findings as she reported them are:

- Virtually every facet of their long lives is formalized and supported by actual and absolute standards — most of them religious codes.

- The extended communal family is the basic social unit, unified by intermarriage, background, and committed to cooperative aid and economic and emotional support.

- The extended family is the primary social, economic, and religious unit. All members of the extended family (or village) are obliged to help the poor and needy families and take care of orphans without respect to lineage. The willingness to help or support their kin is a lesson taught early.

- The oldest male in the family is considered the leader of the family. He has the most rights and influence. He is also the most respected by all the family and villages.

- Boundless commitment to mutual aid is essential to survival. The more family and village ties the individual has, the more secure and influential he or she is considered to be. All members of the family take responsibility for the village elders' safety, comfort, and health.

- The basic feelings of security and stability in life come from the deeply ingrained commitment to aid and nourish each other.

- The elderly show a lack of interest in acquiring "things" or in acting in a competitive manner. To them, life is about people, not economic rivalry.

Longevity in the Caucasus is seen as the result of a rhythmic regularity, social order and repetitive routine. These are critical forces, along with longstanding cultural mores and rigid domestic laws. Individual stress and disagreements are largely absent because they are resolved by the elders, who bring their collective wisdom to family and village problems. Longstanding values and moral codes provide a finite framework — wisdom to live by!

Their diet is simple, consistent, and sensible. The elderly eat a limited number of wholesome foods, mostly dairy, fresh vegetables, and fruits. Largely, their meals are unchanging from month to month, and they have little interest in variety or new taste sensations. Julia Child would not be seen as a valued member of these families. Because theirs is an agrarian society, these simple people of the soil are physically active, walking, climbing, carrying, and digging. Their bodies get exercised daily, 365 days a year.

The elderly are shown great reverence and respect. Their unqualified commitment to volunteer time, talents, and resources to the troubles of the less-fortunate local citizens clearly indicates that altruism is a basic group or family dynamic of their culture. They know that in a sense, they are responsible for the security, welfare, and stability of their extended family.

Dr. John W. Rowe and Dr. Robert L. Kahn confirmed Dr. Benet's Russian study in their MacArthur Foundation study, *Successful Aging*. The well-adjusted senior citizens they interviewed in the United States "spoke of the meaning of being *needed* — and how that keeps them going." And the late Dr. Norman Vincent Peale told of a study by a life insurance company of policyholders who lived to the age of one hundred years or older. One of the survey questions was: "What is the most important thing you have learned in your long life?" The most frequent answer was, "To love thy neighbor as thyself." Dr. Peale concluded: "They live longer because they have freed themselves from deadly negative influences such as anger, hatred, suspicion, guilt, and anxiety." These toxic emotions can lead to cynicism, hostility, and isolation, traits that Dr. Dean Ornish identifies as major components of heart disease, high blood pressure, stroke, and probably cancer.

Dr. Ornish, a noted heart specialist from Harvard, is one of the progressive medical researchers who has been able to reverse heart disease (coronary artery blockage and angina) without scalpel or balloon. In his practice, he drew conclusions about human behavior and how the mind can influence the body. Anger, rage, and hostility are seen as toxic traits that can cause actual damage to functioning body organs. Both overt and concealed rage can sharply elevate blood pressure and increase the buildup of cholesterol in the arteries.

By subjecting his experimental patients to a special lifestyle he has been able to lower blood pressure, bring about actual erosion of arterial plaque, and significantly improve physical endurance. This lifestyle also has helped bring about a more positive mind-set, greater self-esteem, and acceptance of others. To bring about these benefits he puts his patients on a strict no fat, no-cholesterol, fruit-and-vegetable regimen, and he has also designed a mandatory exercise program. One patient, a ninety year-old woman, was able to jog without any bothersome angina, and she also had a significant reduction in arterial plaque. His programs require daily group therapy, daily guided meditation, and self-imaging. Virtually all of these early test patients experienced a notable reduction in plaque and an increase in blood flow; prior to entering Ornish's clinic many of them had been scheduled for open-heart surgery. In his research Dr. Ornish points out that the mind and the emotional exercises aimed at building self-esteem and a positive attitude toward life are essential program elements. When his patients graduate he instructs them all to become involved in some form of helping if they want to live a long and productive life. In his book *Love and Survival*, Dr. Ornish documented the scientific basis for the healing power of intimacy and one of the most intimate of all relationships is gained through the simple act of helping others in need.

Norman Cousins and his UCLA School of Medicine task force studied the relationship between the mind and the immune system and found that emotional stress depresses that vital system and can lead to chronic illness and death. Cousins hoped through his research to discover ways for the mind to send positive, health-sustaining messages to the immune system. These studies highlighted the powerful role of the mind in repairing the body through stress reduction and the enhancement of positive emotions.

That the mind and body cooperate with each other has been documented exhaustively. These scientists are trying to determine which thought processes and actions have a direct and strong impact on the immune system. Not surprisingly, some consider concern for others the most important positive factor.

In a similar study, Harvard doctors David McClelland and Carol Hirshnet discovered that people who watched a documentary about Mother Teresa's work with the dying showed an increase in immunoglobin-A, the body's first line of defense against viral infection. Other movies not focused on compassion had no impact on the immune system. Dr. McClelland also found that people strongly motivated by a drive for power tend to have lower levels of immunoglobin-A than people who were concerned for others. Dr. McClelland concludes: "This suggests that one way to avoid stress and illness associated with a strong power drive is to . . . turn the power drive into helping others."

In the effort to understand how the mind converts ideas and beliefs into biochemical realities, researchers have examined the relationship between social activities, work, and health. Norman Cousins's book describes in detail some ways in which the mind influences biology. A classic instance is the patient who rapidly recovers from a terminal illness after taking only a placebo and, along with it, having a positive belief in the curative powers of the "medication."

The mind can also reduce body temperature and strongly influence the immune system, including the production of T cells. A person's body often physically demonstrates his or her state of mind, so that a troubled mind will "produce" a troubled body. The link between body and emotions is dramatic indeed, and we are becoming more and more capable of determining the impact on our health.

It would be such a wonderful world if doctors, therapists, preachers, and judges suggested, perhaps mandated, that their troubled clients look beyond themselves and become involved in volunteer work and help others, the many benefits to be gained from such efforts can be so rewarding. To those who have set aside a few hours each week to be of assistance to a person or organization that needs help — I commend them. Helping others can become a powerful activity. When you help others there is a good chance that you will gain and grow to become a healthier, more compassionate, and emotionally centered person. Professionals who deal with the human psyche are actively researching the mind/body relationship, and in many different medical research projects, the outcome of the inquiries provides the researchers with real evidence that good deeds and generous giving produce a shower of physical and psychological benefits to the involved volunteer.

Heart specialists like Dr. Dean Ornish and Dr. Herbert Benson and cancer specialists like Dr. Bernard Siegel all say that when we improve our relationships and emotional attitudes, we speed our recovery of health and reduce our risk of life-threatening illnesses. *Psychology Today* recently quoted Dr. Benson on the healing power of giving to others: "For millennia, people have been describing techniques on how to forget oneself, how to experience decreased metabolic rates, lower blood pressure, lower heart rates and other health benefits. Altruism works this way, just as do yoga, spirituality and meditation."

In a special government study of senior-citizen activity in an RSVP test program — a seventy-five city research program — volunteers (and doctors who examined them) reported that in 98 percent of the sites, the physical and mental health of those elders who volunteered to help others experienced significant and measurable improvement in their physical health and mental health.

Most helping projects involve the efforts of a group of volunteers working in close proximity to each other. The locus and the nature of the project, when mixed with social interactivity, keep the elderly involved and active. Investigation shows that continued socializing helps to buffer against isolation, depression, and physical illness. Connecting with other people, bonding and starting new friendships are beneficial rewards.

Philanthropic efforts can break the cycle of stress, social and business pressure, unhealthy relationships, and self-destructive behavior. Working side-by-side with your peers to provide direct assistance or problem-solving can produce a nurturing environment for all who participate. This personal connection with others helps to reinforce one's value and importance. At a point in their lives when many elderly withdraw and reduce their physical and social activity, altruism can truly produce great miracles.

Dr. Dennis Jaffe, in his book *Healing from Within* writes, "Evidence is mounting that over-involvement with oneself, at the expense of the community, leads to psychological dislocation that results not only in anxiety but in various psychological ailments as well." As one medical researcher has broadly commented, "All disease is social in its origin."

The influence of religious devotion has been documented in two studies of Mormons and Seventh-Day Adventists. Researchers found that the risk of cancer among active members of these groups was only about 50 percent as great as that of the average American, the risk of heart attack only 35 percent. Both groups frown on smoking, drinking, and overeating, but they also place great emphasis on practical charity. It may well be that the practice of brotherly love contributes to their members' greater life expectancy as much as do their lifestyles. When researchers in Israel conducted a similar study on a group of Jerusalem residents, they found that those who described themselves as secular had a risk of heart attack four times greater than those who described themselves as religiously orthodox.

Dr. Redford Williams in the book *The Trusting Heart* reports similar results in Evans County, Georgia. Blood pressure levels were lower among residents who frequently attended church than among those who attended less often. Redford cites his colleague Dr. Berton Kaplan, who says, "Many aspects of religious observance could be health enhancing and disease preventing. The world's major religions have as one of their core teachings the injunction to be less concerned with self and more concerned with loving others and treating them well."

The late Dr. Hans Selye has been called the father of stress reduction. Responsible for many early studies of the relationship between stress and illness, he coined the phrase "altruistic ego" to describe a person involved in philanthropic activities. "The love and gratitude we inspire in those we help . . . is a valuable payback," he wrote. "Like stress, love has a cumulative effect." This captures the essence of this book: Sustained good deeds have a cumulative positive effect on our well-being.

A workplace study of 188 companies by David Lewin of the Columbia Business School showed that employee morale was three times greater in companies with a high degree of community involvement than in companies that were uninvolved. Stress has long been a problem in the workplace, and corporate philanthropic activity may be a solution that has been a possibility all along.

Dr. Bernard Siegel in *Love, Medicine and Miracles* predicts an evolving course for the study of the link between altruism and illness: "There is a lack of grant money for this research, but it will surely change as the psychology becomes more widely accepted. Research gradually improves medical care, and I believe that someday we will understand the physiological and psychological workings of love well enough to turn on its full force more reliably."

In a pioneering investigation of 1,500 women volunteers by sociologist Allen Luks, many subjects mentioned the enjoyable physical sensations they experienced while helping others (and for some time afterward). Luks concluded that this "helper's high" reduces the emotional stress that interferes with the body's self-maintenance system. He went on to say, "These stresses cause the adrenal glands to release stress chemicals . . . that increase cholesterol levels that play a role in heart disease, raise blood sugar, and depress the immune system." In contrast, the women Luks investigated spoke of increased energy, a satisfying state of calm, and a feeling of warmth and well-being.

Researchers point to the endorphins, the body's own opiate system, as the source of the emotional and physical high people experience when doing good works; for some, these enhanced feelings last a long time. A number of volunteers claim that since they had begun helping others they experience fewer stress-related ailments and in a nine-year study of relationships between social behavior and the mortality rates of seven thousand Alameda County, California, residents, Drs. Lisa Berkman and S. Leonard Sym found that church members lived longer than those who did not belong to churches.

The ways in which good feelings and increased self-esteem come about were described by Allan Luks in his recent book *The Healing Power of Doing Good*. As a dogged advocate of volunteerism and one who has served well in the independent sector, he has broken fresh ground in describing the physical and emotional benefits derived from giving and volunteering. Luks claims that there are stages that a volunteer or active donor goes through in his or her philanthropic efforts:

Stages

- The "helper's high" is a distinct good feeling about yourself, a central feeling of fulfillment.

- A longer-lasting sense of emotional warmth is stimulated every time the volunteer recalls the event; memory continues to trigger good feelings for days.

- While not fully substantiated, the indications are that the greater or more consistent the giving of time, the greater emotional and physical the feelings are.

Seasoned veterans of volunteerism point to certain conditions that can and often do enhance their physical and emotional feelings. These are:

- Providing your services to one person at a time, where one-to-one, direct contact can be made. This impacts the volunteer's sense of being a valuable and compassionate individual.

- If possible, the individual you help, assist, guide, or counsel should be a stranger to you, not a relative or friend. This factor is difficult to control: if you are in a small community or church, you may know some of the less-fortunate and needy you assist.

- When you offer to help others in a direct manner or become a significant donor, it is important that you let the situation or circumstances evolve — make every effort not to be attached to a single outcome. Many volunteers maintain that they are just messengers, workers for their God; they are not the saviors but merely the humble disciples trying to help one another. There are very few great deeds done by volunteers, just deeds done with sensitive love and concern.

- Some volunteer activities are by their very nature quite intense and dynamic, particularly those that involve solid and continuous one-on-one activities such as mentoring, Big Sister and Big Brother activities, hospice service, and self-help and addiction-recovery efforts.

These emerging findings about the powerful benefits of philanthropic activity point chiefly to volunteers and face-to-face involvement,.but there is a link with financial donations as well. When people give significant amounts of money, personal involvement usually accompanies or follows since interest, concern, and commitment accompany gifts of money.

Instead of the old slogan "Give until it hurts," it seems we should say "Give until you feel great."

A New Path to Emotional Well-Being

God does not work in all hearts alike, but according to the preparation and sensitivity He finds in each.
Meister Eckehart

Struggling with inner conflict is never easy. Many people yearn for a more satisfying life, greater emotional balance, and psychic well-being, but inner happiness and self-acceptance are difficult to achieve and even more difficult to sustain. Life is full of disappointments, frustration, monotony, difficulties at work, family problems, and financial stresses. People become isolated and don't share life's joys easily with one another. As people get older, enthusiasm and satisfaction with life often diminish, often due to declining health.

However, there is one kind of experience that delivers emotional and psychic satisfaction time after time, day after day: helping other people. Volunteer efforts, charitable acts, generosity of spirit, and gestures of compassion all enrich and sustain our lives. Many of the 1,500 women studied by Allan Luks found that helping others took them out of themselves, gave them a greater sense of calm, reduced their anxiety levels, and left them with a greater sense of self-worth.

Volunteering our resources and talents without thought of personal gain showers benefits on us we may never have expected. The "helper's high" can endure long after we are finished and can be relived over and over again in memory.

A stronger, better-defined sense of self emerges through giving: inner approval, feeling more positive about oneself — these are emotional benefits volunteers and donors cite when describing their feelings about acts of generosity. Older people particularly find volunteering helpful as they change and advance in years. The psychologist Eric Erickson says that altruistic behavior enriches what he calls the "integration phase" of a person's life cycle.

Life is all about relationships with others. Many of those we encounter as we go through life may lead us to volunteer work for a cause or issue that touches us deeply. Virtually every kind act has the possibility of producing a favorable outcome for both the donor/helper and the recipient (except perhaps those with deep emotional problems).

Volunteering to help others can be one of those real-life events where we have some control or favorable input. We quickly feel the expansiveness and positive feelings that attend our efforts on behalf of others; when actions are born out of compassion and concern, powerful positive feelings result . Often, our own efforts lead to a bond with co-workers, a strengthening of our self-image, and a more positive outlook. Most of us can recall the good feelings that surfaced after some gifts or donations were delivered to the local orphanage or nursing home at Christmas, partly because of our efforts and partly because of the favorable reactions of the young children; some charitable missions are just more emotionally involved and spiritually satisfying (and humbling), because at Christmas we should let no one be forgotten. From a purely spiritual point of view, what we do for others can truly challenge us to make more room in our life for activities that have such an impact and healthy benefits.

Vernon Wilson of Poquoson, Virginia, gave 1,600 diamonds, rubies, sapphires, emeralds, and other gems valued at $182,000 to the local branch of Habitat for Humanity. When asked about his gift, he said, "I have gotten more satisfaction out of working with the people at Habitat than I ever did with pulling out the gems and admiring them and dreaming about what I could do with them."

Some years ago I visited a man in his early nineties in a Dallas, Texas, retirement home. His mind was as quick as an eighteen-year-old's, his movements as nimble as those of a man half his age. He had "retired" more then twenty-five years earlier and ever since had volunteered as a student counselor at a nearby junior high school. He was still at the school every morning by eight a.m., and his attendance was perfect; he sometimes counseled the children of parents he had helped twenty-five years ago. He gave to those youngsters every day, and in so doing heightened his own physical and mental health. People who retire with no special plans often die within a year of retirement, but those like my friend from Dallas who find a way to share their lives with others seem to live on and on. And the longer they live, the more they have to share and enjoy.

In the Gallup Survey on giving and volunteering, many of those interviewed sought emotional benefits, wanting to feel strong, useful, or needed. They enjoyed doing good works that contribute to an enhanced, more accepting self-image. They viewed their service as a special connection or bond to others, seldom found elsewhere in their lives.

Volunteering and giving enhance self-acceptance. Emotional transference takes place during volunteer activity: in giving love and concern to others we also receive love, gratitude, and acceptance in return. The recently published book *Healthy Pleasures* puts it this way: "We can get a special kind of attention from those we help. This sincere gratitude can be very (emotionally) nourishing. Like the impoverishment of sensuality, we lack healthy doses of genuine appreciation and heartfelt thanks for our good actions. Most of us need such thanks from others, and need to feel that we matter to someone." It follows that the more we help others, the more we gain in self-appreciation and emotional well-being.

Dr. George Vaillant has monitored the progress of a group of Harvard graduates over a forty-year period and reported the resulting wealth of social behavior data in Adaptation to Life. He identifies altruism as one of the rare activities that helped even the most poorly adjusted men in the study group to overcome stress and improve their lives.

In *The Broken Heart: The Medical Consequences of Loneliness,* Dr. James Lynch of the University of Maryland School of Medicine wrote, "'Love your neighbor as you love yourself' is not just a moral mandate. It's a physiological mandate. Caring is biological. One thing you get from caring is that you are not lonely, and the more connected you are to life, the healthier you are." Community and being connected have long been acknowledged as important influences on mental and physical health by the medical and psychiatric professions.

Dr. Dean Ornish, in *A Program for Reversing Heart Disease,* cites self-centeredness, the habitual use of the pronoun "I," and emotional isolation as destructive to emotional and physical health. People need good relationships with other people over the course of their entire lives. Newborn infants do not survive if they are not loved and nurtured, nor do the elderly, and even during our middle years, when we are usually most self-reliant, we are vulnerable. Giving and sharing not only help others; they also give us life.

Sharing and other generous acts are "peak experiences" that can produce far-reaching psychic rewards. In the aforementioned twenty-five-year inquiry into the psychology of optimal experiences, Professor Mihaly Csikszentmihalyi of the University of Chicago identified several conditions as essential to "flow":

- A sense of personal control over circumstances and events.
- A sense that one's skills are adequate to cope with the challenges at hand.
- A goal-directed, rule-bound action system.
- Solid feedback and clear clues as to how well one is performing.
- Intense concentration so there is no attention left over to think about anything irrelevant or worry about personal problems.
- The sense that time is distorted or stands still so that self-consciousness disappears.

I think that giving and sharing squarely meet all these criteria. Helping others provides guidelines, requires sensitivity and adaptive skills, sets goals in helping, and furnishes feedback through the gratitude of those who are helped. In volunteer work, the events are usually controlled by the giver, and the act of helping aids concentration and personal involvement. Volunteer work requires concentration on something beyond one's own problems, and when a volunteer helps another person — as soup kitchen volunteers can attest — time goes so fast that the day sometimes seems to have just begun when it is actually over.

To improve life and enhance self-worth, people need to improve their experiences. No one can buy happiness or contentment, for they are not commodities — they emerge from what we do. Drinking, taking drugs, and overeating often lead to self-loathing and emotional and physical illnesses. Generosity and benevolence, on the other hand, lead to satisfaction and emotional and physical health. We all struggle with both constructive and destructive forces in our personalities. Acts of generosity enhance our feelings of self-worth, which in turn generate greater emotional harmony. A harmoniously ordered mind is the key to a deeper, richer, more enjoyable life.

To have a more balanced life, people need to increase their power to generate emotional rewards. Philanthropy and volunteer work are actions we can take right now to change the direction of our lives. In an age when personal control over circumstances is ever more difficult, an act of sharing gives us a way to direct and shape events. Recent studies with animals have shown that stress diminishes as the perception of being in control increases. Concentrated focus can produce a diminished self-consciousness and a reduction in tension and stress.

We feel good when our efforts succeed and we are thanked for our gifts or help. This feeling of success comes to us in many ways. If the task is financial, a successful fundraising effort can spur greater involvement and pride. Gratitude from those we assist can also be music to our ears: I suspect that Albert Schweitzer had a lot of positive appreciation as well as a mercifully strong physical constitution. I'm sure researchers could find many relationships between giving, gratitude, and inner harmony in the life of this dedicated Nobel Prize winner.

I remember the first campaign I conducted as a professional fundraiser, more than thirty years ago. My client was the Virginia Association of Realtors, the campaign's purpose to endow a Chair of Real Estate at Virginia Commonwealth University in Richmond. The night before the final results of the campaign were to be announced, we were more than $100,000 short of our goal. The chairman of the campaign, Alfred L. Blake Jr., asked me if I thought it would be out of line for him to announce the next day that he personally would make up the difference and put the campaign over the top; there was pride in his voice and there were tears in the eyes of the committee members as he spoke. I also remember the pleasure with which they named the chair in honor of Mr. Blake's father, a pioneering real-estate developer in Virginia. It was, for each of those volunteers, one of the great affirming moments in their lives. For Alfred Blake, it was one of his finest hours.

We all need appreciation, and the more driven among us are often eager for approval; however many of us find little sincere approval in our lives. Volunteer activity for the benefit of others can lead to the sort of genuine approval that benefits us emotionally while we help others. Most Americans are people-oriented, and all of us enjoy having people pay attention to what we say and do. Volunteer effort fosters emotional well-being by empathetic acts, building esteem, and putting our beliefs into practice. As Csikszentmihalyi comments in *Flow: The Psychology of Peak Experience,* "One cannot expect that everyone will become involved in public goals. Some have to devote all their attention to survive in a hostile environment. But life would be harsh indeed if people did not enjoy investing psychic energy in common concerns, thereby creating synergy in the social system."

We are made whole by making others whole. According to Dr. Csikszentmihalyi, people who act out of concern for others markedly improve their lives regardless of their material circumstances. They lead more vigorous, balanced lives, are committed to other people and the environment, are hardly ever bored, and cope well with whatever comes their way. They have structured their lives to benefit from a positive dynamic available to us all: What we do to help others increases self-appreciation and leads to an emotionally rich and rewarding life.

In his book *Power of the Plus Factor*, the late Dr. Norman Vincent Peale wrote, "There is no doubt in my mind that people who care for other people and show that caring in loving unselfish ways most invariably have a strong deep current of the Plus Factor. What we are describing is a person who has discovered the key that unlocks the door to real happiness."

Dr. John Porter, a New York psychotherapist specializing in addiction, points out that "The amazing growth of self-help and recovery groups such as Alcoholics Anonymous, Overeaters Anonymous, and Narcotics Anonymous has largely come about because of the healing powers that operate when one individual or a group of people demonstrates a loving concern for others. When a recovering addict comes to the aid of a confused, desperate newcomer, the helper's self-esteem increases and then is further reinforced by the gratitude of the individual being aided. In essence, people heal each other in a loving and supportive environment. They give of themselves unselfishly and they form a strong bond with the other members of their recovery group. The result of this activity is a restoration to a wholesome and sane life."

Finding Spiritual Harmony

Great Men are they who see that spiritual force is stronger than material force — that thoughts rule the world.
RALPH WALDO EMERSON

Religious belief is a powerful force in American life, unifying, guiding, nourishing and giving meaning to the lives of its followers. Some ninety-nine million Americans attend religious services weekly, and they contribute more than $50 billion each year to religious institutions. It is impossible to discuss philanthropy without reference to religious convictions. Working in the field of philanthropy for many years, I have learned about the power of faith, conviction, and belief. I'm convinced there is a force, an energy, a spirit both in our own lives and external to us that gives purpose to our days on earth. It helps order the mind, bring inner harmony, and shape our highest aspirations. This spirit manifests itself in many ways, but virtually all spirituality is grounded in two vital principles: the need to do good for one another, and the need to love and respect each other.

In most religions the sanctity and value of one's neighbor is paramount. To preserve society and community, compassion, cooperation, and brotherhood are essential. Religion teaches us that it is noble and honorable to cherish and sustain our brothers and sisters. For millions, religious faith is the basic force of life, and actions are praiseworthy if they grow out of a spiritual system of love and respect for others.

Acting to help others has positive effects on our spiritual well-being, and hundreds of people over the years have shared with me the benefits they've derived from giving. In humble and eloquent detail they have described moments of joy, peace of mind, satisfaction, and inner acceptance. When people give to their fellow man, something special happens: They are blessed with an extra dimension of inner harmony.

Philanthropy is a way of life for some people, those dedicated benefactors who are spiritual to the core of their being. Bob Glaze of Dallas, Texas, stays active in business for only one reason: "So I can give more money away." C. Davis Weyerhauser of Tacoma, Washington, gives to more than two hundred charities every year because "This is my way of being a true steward of what God has entrusted to me." John and Donna Crean of Corona Del Mar, California, and Dick and Deanna Freeland of Fort Wayne, Indiana, give the most they can because they are grateful for what has been given to them. These people and many hundreds more like them give away millions every year — not out of obligation, but as an expression of joy and-being.

Of course, the spiritual benefits of giving are subjective and difficult to quantify, but this ambiguity is no different than the one faced every day by doctors and patients. When the doctor asks, "How are you feeling?," the patient's answer is subjective, based on his or her feelings: "I feel fine," or "I feel worse today." In this interchange no precise measurements are made, but the doctor accepts the patient's assessment as valid. In psychology, these interchanges are more complex but essentially the same. The patient describes feelings or emotions in subjective terms: "I feel depressed," or "I feel like a new man." This is the "content" that an entire discipline uses to make diagnoses.

A few years ago a San Francisco psychiatrist and author, Gerald Jampolsky, opened a clinic to treat children and adults with terminal illnesses. He decided not to charge for his services but rather to trust that God would provide; the philosophy of his center is based on giving, not getting for he feels that giving and receiving are, in truth, the same. As he says, "It's amazing how quickly our hearts open up to the presence of peace when we focus all our energy on helping a fellow traveler on the path."

When people tell me that philanthropy has changed their lives, opened up new vistas, brought renewed compassion and love to their spirit, I believe what they say is true. However inarticulate a person's description may be, good deeds enlarge the heart and strengthen the soul. Spirituality and religion are forces that preserve the best in mankind. People aren't born with an abiding faith or peace of mind; they develop it by doing good deeds for others and acting to put their beliefs into practice.

A good deed, what the Torah calls *mitzvah,* connects us to the goodness of God, increases the righteousness in the world, decreases alienation and evil, helps our neighbor, enhances our self-appreciation, and makes everyone — ourselves included — richer.

T·H·R·E·E

EXPANDING YOUR POTENTIAL
FOR HAPPINESS

What the New Findings Suggest

*The central purpose of each life should be
to dilute the misery in the world.*

KARL MENNINGER

Bad news almost always gets better press coverage than good news, so I wouldn't be surprised if you haven't heard the good news about what helping others can do for you.

Drug addiction, for instance, is bad news that gets millions of lines and thousands of hours of media coverage. Governments and organized medicine spend hundreds of millions of dollars to investigate addictions. Scientists, doctors, and therapists study the social and medical issues involved and write countless books, articles, and research papers. Yet all this effort and attention produces only limited results. Millions are also spent to investigate and publicize other crises, such as toxic waste, violence, and child abuse. These problems, too, remain largely unsolved.

Benevolent activity is good news. A handful of researchers with limited funds are now showing that helping others can lead millions of people to improved health and emotional well-being,. But the media attention is minimal, the researchers often have only token support, and the public has yet to receive a comprehensive briefing on the ways our lives can be positively transformed by giving and sharing.

Even the nonprofit world has not realized the full potential of these studies: The $143billion-plus American nonprofit sector has a "product" with powerful healing qualities and needs to say so. These new findings have implications that can radically reshape and extend our expectations of life. If we demonstrate that giving and volunteering improve physical and emotional health, there will be a dramatic increase in philanthropy, with dramatic positive effects on givers and recipients alike.

Most organizations base their appeals on need, perhaps invoking the vague idea that giving and volunteering are "good for the soul" but offering little, if any, concrete evidence. For most, the idea that philanthropy is life-enhancing lies somewhere between a myth and a platitude.

Exactly what are the benefits of giving? They include:

Physical benefits

- Greater longevity
- Significant reduction in toxic stress chemicals in the body (and so less stress)
- Enhanced functioning of the immune system
- Decreased metabolic rate and improved cardiovascular circulation
- Healthier sleep
- Help in maintaining good health

Emotional Benefits

- Increased self-acceptance

- Reduced self-absorption and sense of isolation
- Increased endorphin release (providing a natural emotional "high")
- Reduced inner stress and conflict
- Expanded sense of control over one's life and circumstances
- Increased ability to cope with crises
- Stronger feelings of personal satisfaction
- Improved concentration and enjoyment of experiences
- Enhanced compassion, empathy, and sensitivity to others

Spiritual Benefits

- Greater connection to the God of your understanding
- More receptivity to spiritual guidance
- Stronger involvement in charitable activity
- Heightened sense of appreciation and acceptance of others
- Sustained peace of mind
- Greater clarity about the meaning and purpose of life
- Enhanced quality of life

Considering how many people in our stress-ridden society are looking for physical well-being, emotional buoyancy, and spiritual harmony, there is every reason to believe they will become more involved in helping others if they are given the good news.

There seem to be virtually no negative effects to giving and volunteering except perhaps a drop in the consumption of Valium, Prozac, and sleeping pills. Research will likely establish that the more time, effort, and resources you give, the more benefits you will derive. There may even be a synergistic effect whereby the sum of your efforts is greater than its parts — where, in effect, $2 + 2 = 5$. Already there are people in philanthropy who attest to a synergistic effect among the large and fast-growing elderly segment of our population, nor are the benefits to this group surprising when you consider how much they have to give — time, wisdom, sometimes money, and nearly always motivation to help others.

Americans have recently been changing their ways. Increase in physical exercise, shifts in eating habits, the growth of counseling and psychotherapy, greater interest in meditation, and the proliferation of self-help programs are just a few of the signs that Americans are deeply interested in improving their physical and emotional well-being. Increased philanthropic activity can also bring life-affirming change. The benefits of philanthropy are potential catalysts that can lead to a dramatic upswing in volunteering. With a strong benefit story, nonprofit organizations can tell their volunteers and donors about these new dividends, the "rewards," if you will. Heightened awareness of the power of philanthropy will also broaden respect for giving.

The people whose needs are served by volunteers and donors will also benefit from increased involvement, for more of them will receive more care, concern, and assistance than ever before. A new volunteer tutor might help an immigrant learn English; a local contractor might donate services and materials to help build a summer camp for inner-city Boy Scouts; a restaurant owner might donate food to a homeless shelter. I've seen countless success stories, like that of the volunteer organization City Harvest of New York City, which helps restaurants and markets donate excess food to the hungry.

These are just a few of the changes that can occur if the benefits of philanthropy are made more widely known. Imagine an entire nation devoting at least five hours a week to philanthropic activity — what positive changes that would bring! The reduction in health-insurance claims and lost working days alone would make the program worthwhile. The average American has about thirty-eight hours of optional time each week, so such a change is far from impossible.

Then there are the indirect benefits of greater philanthropic involvement. People who feel good about themselves are more likely to be outgoing and charitable, and helping others is almost certain to bring about a shift in how we view those we serve, making us more compassionate and tolerant. As our willingness to give and share grows, we will also grow spiritually. And when more people volunteer, the gaps left by reductions in government support for education, social, and health services hopefully can be filled and demand for health services among volunteers should decline as people experience a greater sense of well-being and a consequent improvement in their physical health.

Of course, most people do not change their lives easily, and many future volunteers will hold back until the evidence about the benefits of philanthropy is overwhelming. If we are slow to give up smoking and overeating, I don't think we will suddenly stampede to do more good works, but I'm betting it will happen. The nonprofit community can look forward to the day when more and more people come forward spontaneously to serve; by serving others, they will discover that their lives have changed for the better. At this moment, America is being bombarded with popular books about good deeds and loving acts of kindness, such as the *Chicken Soup for the Soul* series. The transformation is well underway!

Yes, You Can Change By Helping Others

*A bit of fragrance always clings to the
hand that gives you roses.*
CHINESE PROVERB

Some people have always understood the benefits of helping others and have led rewarding lives as a result. One such person who has influenced me greatly is Dr. Arthur Frantzreb. Art has raised money for more causes than I can count but does not call himself a fundraiser — he describes himself as a philanthropist. His work is not simply to encourage others to give money, but also to spread the message of each good cause he works for, planting seeds for future work. Another person whose life as a philanthropist has influenced me is Milton Murray, who introduced the "Giving Is Loving" calendars and the "Giving and Sharing: An American Tradition" postage stamp to the world. These calendars, with their daily inspirational quotes, have touched the lives of thousands, including the President of the United States, and who knows how many millions have been influenced by the philanthropic postage stamp?

People active in philanthropy often have a limited view of what happens when they are urged to give to others. As I see it, the public's general reactions upon being asked to help go something like this:

- I'm asked to give time, talent, or other resources to a cause I feel I can support.

- I set aside my time or resources, usually with some sacrifice.

- If my personal involvement with the cause is not very great, I don't really care how my efforts work out. To some extent, my actions are social and I'm filling time or just being with neighbors or friends. (This is especially true if I was motivated to give out of duty or guilt.)

- I have little expectation of anything more than a transient feeling of having done something of merit. (I expect to give without getting anything in return.)

This description seems dour because it's missing the reciprocal benefits. People tend to view giving and volunteering as a one-way transaction, from givers or volunteers to recipients. For the giver or volunteer there may be some fleeting pleasures, minor satisfactions, a vague sense of redemption through good works, but too few of them expect to receive an overflow of physical, psychological, and spiritual good health from their activities.

People establish their perceptions of philanthropy early in life; they assign it value and seldom change their views. For a few, the acts of giving and volunteering are empowering, but for most there is only limited expectation of little more than a token good feeling for a job done, a pledge honored, or one's word kept.

Philanthropy needs a definition that includes all the aspects of giving and sharing, so I offer here a new one that attempts to bring every part of the "philanthropic circle" into a coherent whole: "Philanthropy is the mystical mingling of a joyful giver, an artful asker, and a grateful recipient." All three — the giver, asker, and recipient — benefit from the philanthropic experience. All three are part of the philanthropic circle.

Until now, the call to help others has usually ignored an important element: proof that philanthropic activity enhances the giver's physical and emotional well-being. Now that evidence, that keystone, is being put into place. The new research delivers a clear and direct message: the more you give and share, the more you benefit.

At last we have some concrete measurements of the return on our investments of time and resources. These dividends are not material; they involve physical and emotional states that money can seldom buy, qualities that enhance our lives. These benefits are fairly easy to grasp, uncomplicated, and easy to predict. They function in a simple cause-and-effect manner, much like a family doctor's familiar counsel ("Follow a healthy diet, exercise regularly, reduce stress, and you'll get better").

I wish the benefits of philanthropic involvement carried an unconditional guarantee, but as with the doctor's advice, there's no sure thing or quick fix. Consistent and frequent involvement in giving and sharing can indeed transform people, but only if they follow sensible guidelines for living. The hyperactive, driven, overly competitive executive probably can't find much time in his schedule for more activity, so rather than devote many hours, he should give himself fully to one or two causes. It is his unique character and ability that count, not how many hours he gives. People need to give *who* they are, not just *what* they have or can do!

To be with people, to be involved in a cooperative effort, to lose your self-awareness to a task or mission is my idea of how to truly benefit from giving and sharing. To quote the late Mother Teresa on the subject volunteers: "I just ask them to come and love the people, to give their hands to serve them and their hearts to love them." The benefits of philanthropy are cumulative and come from sustained efforts. You can't separate the benefits from the giving any more than you can attain them by pursuing them with no genuine concern for the cause.

Time has a great deal of value. Many people lead busy, involved, active lives. They have to operate on many levels: family, community, business, recreational, and social. Many are overcommitted, and some lead very intense pressured lives. I know they are sorry that they can't do more. Both husband and wife often work, and time together as a family is all the more valuable because it is difficult to find.

However the only way to take advantage of the benefits of sharing and giving is to find time and do it. You should consider setting aside time to become involved and committed to a cause that matters to you. I can hear your lament already: "But I just don't have the time." Consider the irony: you are striving for success and security in order to find physical, emotional, and spiritual well-being. Philanthropic activity can give you precisely what you're seeking and not finding at work — perhaps it might be a better use of your time?

Limited vision is a barrier to harmonious living. People can be so bedeviled by the demands of the moment that they can't order their own lives satisfactorily. The squeaky wheel gets the attention; the roar of ambition drowns out the impulse to set aside time to help others. The demands of society are continuous and always expanding, but so are the many opportunities to help others. The rewards of philanthropy wait patiently for you to claim them — the only question is, when?

Some will postpone any effort to begin helping others until they have conquered the material world, but sometimes life seriously reduces people's options and they may find themselves overworked, overwhelmed, or in poor health. Sometimes a person who puts off sharing ends up the recipient of philanthropic services before he or she has ever tasted the fruits of giving. Many a homeless family in a shelter tonight never thought they would ever be on the receiving end of philanthropy. Ironically, the way back for many of them will involve giving one of the few things they now have, time, but time and money given earlier — and the joy such giving would have brought — might have been the turning point that kept a family from the ranks of the homeless.

I believe that interest and participation in philanthropy will expand slowly, keeping pace with discoveries about the benefits to be derived from philanthropic involvement. I wish it could happen faster, but until more people know about these discoveries, they will hesitate. Once the story gains momentum, though, I think it will also grow and spread like a late-summer grass fire fanned by a strong wind.

Of all the things that work against this good news, impatience — the desire for a "quick fix" — is the most dangerous. We expect immediate, almost magical results from our plans to help others; sincere effort and dedication can produce remarkable results, but not overnight. We need to be willing to wait and trust the process.

The benefits giving and sharing can deliver are the same ones most of America seeks. Giving offers you a new and better path with a great deal to gain but little in the way of sacrifice. This is a fresh new message. The more you give of yourself, the happier, healthier, and more contented you will become. Moreover, you will experience these benefits at the same time as you take your journey into sharing and giving. It is not a magic odyssey down a yellow brick road but a real-world encounter promising enhanced health and emotional harmony. I'm convinced that if you use the approaches, guidelines, and techniques set forth in this book, you will have a much better chance to experience a complete range of benefits.

For some the promises have already come true. You have probably seen this in your own community. Certain people radiate a special kind of well-being or spiritual harmony. One such quiet man of great kindness and dedication is Dr. Oliver Sacks, who tells of his efforts to help the mentally ill in the award-winning book and movie *Awakenings*. For years he had been caring for "lost souls"men and women suffering from a destructive form of encephalitis; many of his patients had been institutionalized for decades. They awakened his compassion, and in his book he describes how his caring led to new personal tenderness and "awakening" to life. Those he treated for years became his teachers and friends. His is a powerful story of how philanthropy can change your life.

There are people like Dr. Sacks in your town. Single out these quiet (or noisy) philanthropists who are changing the world. When you find them, get to know them. They may have much to teach you.

The residents of Somerville, New Jersey, will never be the same since a quiet seventy-two year-old neighbor, Eleanor Boyer, stepped forward to announce that she was giving all of the $11.8 million ($8.5 million after taxes) she had won from the New Jersey lottery to her church and other charities in her town. Although in truth she could have used some of the money, she adamantly said she did not need it. How much of your lottery winnings would you give away? Eleanor answered "all." It just might be that her example of genuine love for others will have an influence on you as it may have on Frank Capaci of Steamwood, Illinois. After winning $104.3 million after taxes in the Powerball lottery Frank said playfully to his friends, "I got a lot of money. I will donate it — you wait your turn." If you won, what would you say?

Maximizing Your Pleasures and Joys

We must not only give what we have;
we must also give what we are.
Desire Mercier

Americans are grudgingly coming to realize that money and power alone don't produce happiness. Materialism will always be attractive, but growing numbers of young and old are moving toward a more spiritually centered life. Philanthropic activity is a high road to enjoyment and happiness.

Every day I see people becoming more and more committed to causes that put their beliefs about the dignity of man and the best course for society into action. I see people becoming more willing to make things happen. I'm sure that part of this shift comes from a recognition that happiness cannot be attained passively. It requires energy and involvement.

Few in our society ever attain great wealth, but those who do often display as much warmth, compassion, and wisdom as the rest of us. It is remarkable how many people who have amassed fortunes of billions or hundreds of millions of dollars set aside large portions for philanthropic purposes. They find great satisfaction in making a gift of millions to a favorite cause and seeing the goals of that cause attained.

Those of us with more limited resources can gain the same measure of happiness when we share what we have; sometimes miracles just happen. I am reminded of a man in Richmond, Virginia, who gives away more money each year than he makes (his salary is under $20,000). When asked how he does it, he always says, "I just do it and it always works out okay." The very heart of philanthropy is commitment, the willingness to support a cause for a long time with whatever resources you have. The greater your personal involvement, the greater the possibility of expanding your happiness and satisfaction.

A central theme of this book is how to make the most of the pleasures of giving and sharing. Most of us believe there is some benefit to compassionate acts, though the rewards may seem momentary and fleeting, but many don't experience the physical and emotional benefits from active involvement at all. I hope I can reveal a path to joy and happiness. This path is not easy to describe, but it does exist.

Every organized religion teaches its followers that happiness comes in part from loving and serving our neighbors. Many philosophers have said that happiness comes from right actions, good deeds, and compassion, that our self-discovery, self-esteem, and fulfillment grow as we share with (and support) others. This has been the teaching of great men for centuries, from Moses and Buddha to Jesus and Mohammed, but in the absence of real reasons to follow this wise counsel, its practical application in people's lives has been limited.

In industrial societies, many have come to believe that happiness is achieved through amassing wealth and power. In tribal and agrarian societies, interdependence and sharing are more apt to be seen as the essential aspects of survival, with a happy person being one who contributes to the well-being of the group. Our new knowledge of the benefits of philanthropy can help bridge the gap between these two types of society: It can, indeed, contribute to mutual understanding and world peace.

Happiness is self-generated, something we set in motion for ourselves. Some of the best experiences in my life occurred when I stretched my talents and capacities to the limit trying to accomplish something for others. In particular I remember what my life was like before I was a giver and what it is like today. Some years ago I decided to stop talking about giving and become a participant. I set aside $3,500 to set up a foundation; I did not have large amounts of money and so the only way for this foundation to grow was for me to contribute to it each year.

I have contributed every year since then, and the results have been phenomenal. First, the foundation itself has grown to more than $150,000, even though each year it gives away a healthy portion of its assets. (My goal is to build the foundation to at least one million before I die.) Second, I have grown more spiritual in my outlook toward life and others, and in this new spirituality I have found peace of mind. And third, my income has grown each year since I set up the foundation, which has made it possible for me to give more away each year. An old expression

I had never understood before has become part of my life: "You can't out-give God."

The more I give, the more I have; maybe that is what that "saint" in Richmond, Virginia, finds as he gives away more than he makes. I haven't come to that point yet, but the goal is one I may reach as my foundation continues to grow from my annual investments. And, naturally, I will give to the foundation as large a portion of the royalties from this book as the tax laws will allow.

I'm not one of those proselytizers who urges people to give away their wealth, abandon their families, and go work among the sick and the destitute. I only suggest that since happiness comes from making others happy, an investment of time, effort, and resources toward helping others will probably lighten your burden and produce sustaining joy in your life. Until now, many of us weren't sure just what we might look forward to getting from our giving. Scientists have given these uncertain dimensions some real definition.

All of us have an opportunity to increase our enjoyment of life while at the same time bringing benefits to others. The principle of giving to live asserts that if you increase your philanthropic activity, more benefits and rewards will come to you than to those you assist or the causes you champion. You have it in your power to test this formula any time you desire if you are open to possibilities and willing to move along the Giving Path.

If you are skeptical, you might try the ninety-day "Give to Live Challenge." First, go to your doctor and get a complete physical, then get involved with your favorite cause once or twice a week (four to eight hours per week) for ninety days. When the ninety days are up, see your doctor again and see if there have been any changes. Most importantly, ask yourself how you feel. I'm willing to bet that you will see growth in self-appreciation, physical well-being, and spiritual harmony. Why not try it?

If the ninety-day challenge works for you, extend it to six months or a year. Set aside the time, develop a program, and start experimenting with it. As Abraham Lincoln once observed, "Most people are about as happy as they make up their minds to be." What he didn't foresee was that real contentment and joy could come out of making up our minds to help others.

Dr. Robert Schuller, the founding pastor of the Crystal Cathedral in Garden Grove, California, wrote in his bestseller *The Be Happy Attitudes*, "We all know people who do not lie, kill, steal . . . [who] live a life of ease, comfort and noninvolvement. They appear to be kind and gentle and we are tempted to judge them to be 'loving people.' But real love involves commitment. If they take no daring risk, they're good — but for what?" When Dr. Schuller asked psychologist Dr. Joyce Brothers what our deepest need was, she replied, ". . . human beings need love. It doesn't have to be the love between a man and woman. It can be love of mankind." Sharing and caring are primal human needs, and the life that fulfills these is beneficial to the giver and receiver alike.

The Leap of Faith

*What shall I do with my life? How much am I willing
to give of myself, of my time, of my love?*
ELEANOR ROOSEVELT

A growing body of evidence points to philanthropy as beneficial to people who give their time, energy, talent, and
resources. This new evidence is still more directional than
conclusive and while the results I have shared with you are
exciting and make a great deal of sense, but the whole story
has not yet been told: Beyond all the research, lie your own
philanthropic experiences and those of other extraordinary
individuals, people who have chosen to devote their lives to
a cause. These people often radiate a passion and seem to
have a richer sense of life.

I think of Paul Meyer, a founder of S.M.I. in Waco,
Texas, who has made millions and each year gives millions
away. He uses his considerable energy to make money
then takes that same energy and money and uses it to help
others. What is amazing is that many people like Paul
reach an age where infirmity would normally restrict them,
but they don't slow down — they keep on giving, and even
giving more, year after year: think of that ninety-year-old
from Dallas who counsels junior high students.

Or what about Charles Feeney, a businessman from
New Jersey, who for a decade anonymously gave away more
than $600 million through his two charitable foundations?
At least $3.5 billion more has been turned over to his foun-
dations, which makes him one of the most generous philanthropists of all time. Having made all this money himself,
he has kept very little for himself: he does not own a house
or car, he flys coach, and he told the *New York Times* when

his anonymous largesse was exposed, "Money has an attraction for some people, but nobody can wear two pairs of shoes at the same time."

These people have found something special. You can't help admiring them or wanting to be around them, for their positive energy is infectious, and they give everyone around them a new sense of the goodness of life. I see people like these often in my work, and they inspire me. They remind me how much a single person can do and how easy it is to change the world and change your own life. They are an amazing testimonial to the principle of giving to live.

In telling this story of the benefits of giving and sharing, I have presented a broad range of promising scientific inquiries and the stories of some wonderfully inspiring, dedicated people who give unselfishly and live longer and more rewarding lives as a result. Providing a backdrop to all of this is the collective wisdom of great philosophers who have consistently urged people to give of themselves, to fill their lives with good acts. Great rewards can come to those who consistently care and share.

Do you really believe that your participation in philanthropic activities can bring you greater well-being and a longer life? Are you convinced that there is more to philanthropy than meets the eye? Some of you may say, "Well, what you've presented makes sense, but I want more proof. I want some more scientific evidence." Others may simply not believe, or may suspect that these powers of philanthropy can enrich everyone *except* themselves.

Well, you will never know unless you try. Are you willing to take that proverbial leap of faith with only limited evidence? Can you set aside your fears and make the practice of giving more central in your life? Are you willing to act and trust that positive results will follow?

One way to begin: Ask yourself how important these new benefits might be to you. What are you willing to do to live longer, to feel better physically and emotionally? Most of us value these ends highly enough that we will not simply reject them out of hand, so if you look carefully at what I'm proposing, you may conclude that the risks are well worth the potential benefits. Consider giving a few hours a week, donating money or resources, getting involved in a cause. The "tenfold increase" mentioned in the Bible may arrive in the form of health, emotional well-being, or spiritual harmony. There are no guarantees, but what else has brought you these dividends recently?

I am not trying to trick anyone into doing anything. I truly believe in the powers of philanthropy and I hope to both inform and inspire you. The new research on giving has tremendous ramifications, but how meaningful this approach to living can be in your own life is entirely up to you. It might cut into some of your social time, your television time, or your fishing time; it is a rare individual, however, who can't free up a few hours a week for volunteer work. Most of us spontaneously help friends and neighbors, and what I'm suggesting is involvement in the world of philanthropy: working with a church group to feed and house homeless people, teaching youngsters how to swim, or raising funds for a senior citizens' center. There is no lack of opportunity.

Another way to get a feel for what participation can mean is to spend a little time talking to people who have been touched by the powers of philanthropy. Pick a non-profit organization and ask the director to introduce you to one of their volunteers or donors; sit down with this person and ask him or her to tell you what giving and volunteering has done for them, and when you get home, drop me a letter and let me know what they said. Send your letters to:

> Douglas M. Lawson
> Douglas M. Lawson Associates, Inc.
> 545 Madison Avenue
> New York, NY 10022
> Voice: (800) 238-0004
> E-mail: doug@douglawson.com

I will use your stories in my research, and you can use these stories to make your own life-changing decisions.

I'm old enough and experienced enough to know that this message is at odds with powerful forces in our society. In this age of self-interest it isn't easy to capture the attention of the millions scrambling for wealth, prestige, and power. Achievement, material gain, and security are drives as ancient — and as seductive — as our concern for one another. Thousands of years ago, charitable acts were also locked in conflict with people's desire for wealth and power. At the dawn of civilization people possessed no scientific information that supported the physical, psychological, and spiritual benefits of philanthropic acts, yet even in those early days they instinctively knew that being a benefactor had magical qualities. The Torah, the works of Jesus, the teachings of Plato and Mohammed all invest philanthropic activity with a special grace — a grace that needs to be rediscovered in every generation.

People, as a rule, don't like change. We develop daily rhythms, structure our activities, and resist change, for change can bring stress and dislocation. Even when faced with evidence that changes need to be made, we balk: ask any doctor about the difficulties they have in getting their patients to quit smoking or cut down on fat in their diet. Too many of us ignore or resist good counsel until we find ourselves in life-threatening situations. The medical evidence may be all but conclusive, yet many still ignore it. We will doubtless do the same with our new knowledge about philanthropy; only time will tell.

People will not easily alter their perceptions of giving. Some who give their time, talent, and treasure don't get much pleasure and satisfaction from their benevolence. Perhaps their involvement has become automatic rather than personal. Some people refer to their volunteer efforts as sacrificial, and some activities lose their energy and appeal over time. It doesn't have to be this way. I will later describe approaches anyone can adopt to reduce or eliminate this malaise, which some call emotional fatigue or burnout. Renewal is possible, and the remedies to burnout are practical and sensible.

While there are no known disadvantages to increased giving except overextension, the benefits won't always be visited upon you overnight. Most likely they will blossom as you deepen your resolve, increase your involvement, and change your perceptions. Philanthropic activities don't provide a quick fix for a life badly out of balance, but acts of sharing and caring nourish the giver.

I can't tell you how long it will take or how quickly you will experience the powerful benefits of philanthropy, but I'm convinced that it will happen. You may need a "leap of faith" in the beginning, but all the elements needed to produce a small miracle in your life are already in place — to begin, you need only believe it can be so, and then start.

Why not take the ninety-day *"Give to Live Challenge"* now? And when the ninety days are up, drop me a line and let me know how you feel about your life; you just might be amazed.

F·O·U·R

CREATIVE WAYS TO GIVE

Render Unto Caesar or Charity

There is little hope for democracy if the hearts of men and women in democratic societies cannot be touched by a call to something greater than themselves.

MARGARET THATCHER

Our nation is a rich nation both in terms of resources and human enterprise. For the past several years our economy has helped us solidify our financial goals with very little financial turbulence. Government debt and unemployment have been mercifully manageable; personal income taxes have been reasonable. Just about all our major economic indicators point to financial success, regardless of the stock market's gyrations.

Let's go back in time, for a minute, to the era that welcomed world peace and the chance to create a positive, secure home and environment: the years 1946 to 1963. The maternity wards of America's hospitals delivered a bumper crop of babies and now in the final decade of the Twentieth century, as the "boomers" thrive in their own businesses, they will soon be the recipients of inheritances and bequests as senior family members pass away. Now baby boomers with "deep pockets" will be expected to use their windfalls to sustain their special philanthropies. The sum total of the treasures being transferred to baby boomers is staggering in size — more than $7 trillion. One way to think about this phenomenon is to note that the top 30 percent of inheritors will each be given about $1.3 million — certainly a bit more than "spending money."

Individual fortunes have been increasing at a rapid rate in recent years. Financial analysts have released calculations that estimate that there are about one hundred individuals who have amassed personal fortunes in excess of $1 billion. Leading the parade is the young and dedicated computer whiz, Bill Gates, with an estimated net worth of $40 billion; other billionaires include George Soros, Warren Buffet, and Ted Turner. A recent review of personal fortunes estimates that there are now about 250,000 multimillionaires. And, as you probably know, America's wealth is heavily concentrated, with the top 1 percent owning some 33 percent of America's wealth. The next 9 percent of our population owns about another 33 percent of the wealth, while the vast majority (90 percent) owns the final 33 percent.

How about you: Have you created a sizable estate? Or have you accumulated a more modest personal estate but still care about how it is used? Perhaps now is the time to decide how you plan to distribute your wealth. If you are over fifty and have any kind of assets you hope to pass on to your children, relatives, and charity, I urge you to begin conversations with a tax accountant, estate lawyer, or financial planner.

I just know that you have worked hard to accumulate your estate, whatever its size, and I'm sure you have definite ideas about its disposition. Well, your federal and state governments also have ideas about how they would like to use your assets. If you miss a beat in estate planning, there is little doubt about the IRS's response — they will become the "charity" you contribute to, whether you like it or not! If you don't want a large piece of your estate used to bail out a poorly managed bank or buy a $700 wrench for the Air Force, please draw up a charitable estate plan with expert advice, and implement it; better to fund a shelter for the homeless than a congressional junket to the south of France. You have in your power the possibility to choose the charities you wish to support with your hard-earned funds, but to do this you must plan your estate *now, — not later,* when it is too late.

If it hasn't happened already, someday soon your minister or favorite charity representative is going to ask you for a sizable gift. And they should; it is their responsibility to you to ask. While you may be uncomfortable with thoughts of your own demise, unfortunately it *will* happen. It will do you no harm, and probably much good, to plan to give a portion of your estate to a cause or institution you strongly believe in. Even if your assets are now tied up in property, stocks, or a business and you cannot make an immediate gift, you can still do some future planning. There are ways that a gift can be made now so that it doesn't diminish your current income. In fact, many estate gifts can enhance your income for the rest of your life.

Careful planning can ensure that most — perhaps all — of your estate funds end up going where you want them to go. There is a rare moment in every person's life when they have the opportunity, as Bob Buford in his book *Half Time* puts it, to move "from financial success to personal significance." That opportunity in an affluent society such as ours is probably yours today. What do you intend to do about this magic moment? Is *financial success* really what you want to be remembered for — or is *personal significance* more likely what you desire. I hope it is the latter, and sharing what you have with others is your clearest path to that goal. If you are like some who are already receiving windfalls, the idea of putting the money back into circulation is important. Some may wish to express gratitude for their blessings. To repeat a simple thought: "He who dies rich has missed the point of life." This is a something we might all ponder.

Ways to Give

Money is important in the getting and the giving,
not in the having.
JOSEPH JACOBS

Many people believe that the most precious gift we have to give to others is our time. All of us have the same amount of this human resource every day of our lives. Rich or poor, young or old, male or female, we still have the same amount of time every day. The question for all of us is not do we have time, but how are we best to use it?

When I was a struggling young married divinity student, I did not have sufficient money one Christmas to give my son, Sam, the presents I really wanted to buy for him, so I gave him a Christmas card on which I wrote these words: "This year, Sam, I am going to give you one hour of my time every day." The first day after Christmas Sam stood in front of me and said, "Dad, can we have *our* time now?" Never once during the year ahead did he ever call it *Hour* time. He forgot about the one hour immediately and was satisfied with the only symbol of love I had to give — my time. In those "our time" moments with Sam I discovered something that had always eluded me: happiness. And I discovered it by first giving it to my little boy. I made him happy by giving him the only thing I really had, and as I brought him happiness, he made me happy and more loving.

Beyond our time which we can share with others, we can also have our talents. Some of the greatest gifts ever donated have been in the form of talents. Are you an accountant? Why not consider offering some of your services to a struggling nonprofit in your community? Are you a former teacher? How would it feel to be sharing your teaching skills with a tutoring program conducted by a local charity in your town? We all have talents to give; it is just a question of whether we are willing to share them with others as a gift rather than as a service for which we charge. The pay for a gift of talent is higher than for a talent with a price tag on it. Only the giver knows that this is true.

Our time and talents are something that we all can share with others. Some of us are also blessed with treasures in the form of monetary assets and funds that are over and above those we might ever need. What we do with these excess funds can make or break our future lives; many an alcoholic or otherwise addicted rich person knows of what I speak. In an affluent society such as ours, too much money can "kill" us or it can be the catalyst for bringing into our lives the blessings of health, happiness, and a long life which givers experience every day.

Assuming that our choice is not to "destroy" ourselves with our money, how can we get on a path where we can find creative and meaningful ways to give it to others? It is really not all that difficult, but it will take some careful attention to learning the various strategies that we can creatively use to bring meaningful gifts to others, particularly those in need.

Before reviewing the various ways to make financial contributions, we should first understand that all charitable gifts in the United States are divided into two primary categories: *deferred gifts* and *present gifts*. Deferred gifts go to charities at a future date determined by either the term of years set up by the donor or by the death of the donor, or another person. Present gifts are received by charities now in the form of outright contributions of cash, stocks, bonds, or property. Present gifts are the most tax-effective way to give, but deferred gifts do offer some tax benefits as well as benefits to the donor's family.

Present Creative Ways to Give

The simplest present way to give is by making a contribution by check which is deductible from your income taxes — up to 50 percent each year; credit cards are also widely used today for present gifts. When the stock market is booming, as it often is, appreciated stocks become an excellent resource to give. Stocks and bonds can be deductible up to the full market value of these financial instruments once the stocks or bonds have been unconditionally delivered to the donee or the donee's agent. Real estate can also be deeded to charities as present gifts, as can promissory notes. The most common way to make a creative present gift is by making a pledge to a nonprofit which can be satisfied through payments of cash or other property over a period of time usually no longer than three to five years.

Deferred Creative Ways to Give

Whereas present gifts almost always give the best tax deduction to you, the donor, deferred gifts are the best way to plan for your future and that of your family. From both an income and a tax point of view, there are many creative ways to give deferred gifts, but the following eight are the most widely used by donors. It is important as you contemplate using one or more of these eight deferred methods of giving that you first contact your accountant or lawyer for advice and counsel, especially regarding taxes.

1. **Charitable Remainder Unitrusts.** When a donor uses a charitable remainder unitrust as his or her deferred giving instrument, certain benefits immediately accrue to the donor. First, no capital gains taxes are paid on the money or property put into the unitrust, which can consist of cash, stocks, bonds, and real estate. Second, the property invested in the unitrust is invested basically tax-free, more or less like a permanent IRA, Keogh, or 401-K plan except in the case of unrelated business income. Third, income of 5 percent or more is paid from the unitrust to the donor for life and to a second person for life if it is a two-life unitrust. And fourth, the donor gets a tax deduction now even though the corpus does not go to the designated charity or charities until the death of the donor and the death of the second person (if it is a two-life unitrust).

Charitable remainder unitrusts are one of the most frequently used deferred giving vehicles in the United States. It is truly a way to not only create an excellent income-producing retirement fund for you and your loved ones which does not force you to deplete the corpus during your lifetime, but it is also a way to give substantial sums to charities of your choice in the future.

2. **Charitable Remainder Annuity Trusts.** Operating much in the same manner and with similar benefits as

a unitrust, the charitable remainder annuity trust differs primarily in the way that income is distributed to the donor. The unitrust uses a percentage, whereas the annuity trust uses a specified annuity amount that is paid each year to the donor or the person who is designated as the second life.

3.   **Gift of Property with a Retained Life Interest.** One very creative way to give is to deed property such as a personal residence or a vacation home to a charity while retaining a life interest in it. Simply put, this type of a gift allows the donor to benefit from a sizable tax deduction now while retaining his or her right to use the home or vacation property for the rest of his or her life in the same manner as before the gift was made.

4.   **Lead Trust.** A way to get immediate funds to the nonprofit of your choice and to pass on major funds to your heirs later — all with substantial gift and estate tax savings — is through a lead trust. Although it is much more complicated than it appears, in most basic terms the donor puts a sum of money into a lead trust that will give income to the nonprofit for a period of years (ten or more). A simple example: a donor commits to giving one million dollars to a charity over the next ten years; this is accomplished through a lead trust, which the donor creates by placing one million in assets into the trust. The lead-trust funds are then invested to achieve an income stream annually of at least 10 percent or more. This income allows the lead trust to pay $100,00 a year to the nonprofit for ten years. The lead trust corpus is then passed on to the donor's heirs with accompanying gift- and estate-tax savings.

5. **Bargain Sales.** An excellent way to give property (such as real estate and tangible personal property, including cars or yachts) is to enter into a bargain sale of your property to a charitable organization for less than the property's fair value. In effect, the donor makes a tax-deductible contribution equal to the difference between the selling price and the property's fair value. This is a creative way to get some cash for your property while receiving the remainder of the value of the property in the form of a tax deduction.

6. **Charitable Gift Annuities.** Another excellent vehicle for maturing adults to obtain a better rate of return on their savings while ultimately making a gift to a charity is the charitable gift annuity. The donor purchases a gift annuity contract from a charity with an excellent guaranteed annual rate of return; at the time of the purchase the donor can deduct a portion of the funds used to purchase the gift annuity. Like other deferred giving methods of giving, the donor receives tax benefits now, guaranteed extra income in the future, and a major gift to a charity of choice at the donor's death. This is almost too good to be true! But then again, creative giving can be more exciting than you could ever imagine!

7. **Life Insurance.** Another important way to give a deferred gift is through the purchase of life insurance. This is an excellent way for a young donor to leverage his or her youth with a relatively impressive life insurance policy that will pay out to the charity of choice a major future gift far exceeding what the donor can afford at the time the policy is purchased. All premium payments to a life insurance policy where a charity is the beneficiary are tax deductible,

and if you already have a paid-up policy that you would like to donate to a charity, all the premium payments you have made to purchase the policy are tax deductible at the time it is gifted to the charity.

8. **Gifts by Will.** Testamentary gifts by will are not as dynamic, tax-wise, as present gifts, but gifts by will are a way for your heirs to escape some inheritance taxes while making it possible for the charities of your choice to receive major gifts at your death. You are deprived of the joy of giving those gifts now as a donor, but you have the pleasure of knowing that at your death you, not the government, are the one who determines the final distribution of your hard-earned financial estate.

All of us are blessed with financial assets we can share with others if we choose to. The widow and her mite and the millionaire and his million are equal in the eyes of God. It does not, finally, really matter how much you give, but if you do choose to give it is important that you give it creatively. Ted Turner chose to give $1 billion, $100 million for each of ten years. And that is not all that he has. The widow two thousand years ago decided to give all that she had, "a mite". If that mite had been invested creatively back then, it would today be worth more than the billion Ted Turner is giving away. To get on the Giving Path today, we need to be creative in our giving, regardless of the amount we choose to share with others.

F·I·V·E

LIVING ON THE GIVING PATH

The Giving Path

There never was a person who did anything worth doing,
who did not receive more than he gave.

HENRY WARD BEECHER

In my seminars and lectures I like to review the natural course of a life of sharing, which I call *The Giving Path*. The urge towards generosity usually starts early in life, then flows along a continuum with early family instruction at one end and a naturally sensitive and spontaneous benevolence at the other. As I see it, the Giving Path unfolds something like this:

- *Beginnings:* Early parental teaching and examples help form childhood attitudes towards giving and money.

- *Reinforcement:* In early schooling teachers, parents, and religious instructors help form an "emotional set" about giving, sharing, philanthropy, and the value attached to money and possessions. Social responsibility is also formed at this stage.

- *Actualization:* Children begin to experience giving and sharing themselves. These early experiences, sometimes wonderfully confusing and embarrassing, make lasting impressions on children. The extended family helps encourage and support children's generous impulses.

- *Independence:* Young people begin to help those in need, freely using their own resources as new but increasingly vested members of the community.

- *Intensification:* Teenagers and young adults commit themselves to causes requiring volunteer service, active identification, and giving.

- *Maturity:* Adults make a wholehearted investment in a cause, inspiring spiritual kinship. Large gifts and bequests are often the natural result of this devotion.

There is no single Giving Path. Everyone's life has twists and turns, lapses, defections, disenchantments, and resistances. Compassion and selflessness develop very early in life and largely determine adult behavior. Willingness, devotion, levels of participation, and degrees of commitment are finely honed over a lifetime, but it is early experiences that exert the most powerful influence over everyone's adult patterns of volunteering and giving. Conviction, resiliency, and passion for a cause usually spring from early, sensitized encounters.

I have heard H. Ross Perot, who rose from very poor circumstances to become a billionaire, talk about his mother feeding the homeless during the Depression. No wonder Perot became a giver as an adult because he learned it at his mother's knee when he was young and poor. The same is true for me: My father and mother, who were lower-middle-class at best, were consistently generous. They gave regularly to their church, and when neighbors and strangers alike needed help, no matter who they were my parents were ready to give. I probably learned everything I know about philanthropy before I ever left home, and chances are most of you did too.

Some Live to Give

At a lecture I gave in San Diego connected with the first edition of *Give to Live*, I had the privilege of meeting Cecil Green, one of the founders of Texas Instruments. He was in his nineties and had already given away more than 150 million dollars to causes all over the world. I gave him a copy of my book and he later sent me a book about his life and that of his wife, Ida. In the book he inscribed these words to me:

> I really agree with what you say in your book *Give to Live*. I guess the way Ida and I would have put it, however, is that we "lived to give."

According to one challenging philosopher of the past: "He who dies rich has missed the point of life." In a world that seems totally bent upon accumulation and acquisition of wealth, many have wondered whether the rich and near-rich have time to really be concerned with some of the gross iniquities of life: Are they compassionate? Amidst the high stakes players, do they take time to smell the flowers and perhaps — hopefully — look into the ways they might be of meaningful help to their less fortunate neighbors or utilize their wealth to help the sick or illiterate? In this nation there is no lack of opportunity; unfortunately the public is somewhat indifferent to the benevolence of the rich and super-rich. So many high-powered, driven, successful people are often considered to be too busy making deals and consolidating their "power plays" to be genuinely concerned about the many educational, social, medical, and housing problems that desperately require public and private assistance.

However many successful people, like Mark Fleckenstein, are not too busy making money to help. Mark, a millionaire, startled the residents of San Antonio, Texas, by standing on the street corner and giving $100 bills to homeless people. He wanted to help them today, not tomorrow, and he wanted to help them in a tangible way that made a difference. Mark has since decided to make most of his contributions to the homeless directly to agencies that can get more good out of his money, but he still wants his money to help others — and he wants it to help others now.

The most common view about wealthy individuals is that they are all philanthropists to some extent but that they keep a healthy reserve for a rainy day. There is an edgy suspicion that the very rich give far too little of their largesse to worthy causes. In a sense, the command to give charitably weighs heavily on them because many of them lead high-profile lives, while in many ways the very rich are no different than you and me, it is true that their responsibilities are usually greater than most.

One wealthy family that for more than forty years has given away 50 percent of their income annually is John and Donna Crean of Orange County, California. Recently John retired from Fleetwood Enterprises, which he founded, by selling his 14 percent stake back to Fleetwood for $176 million cash. Without missing a step, he put 50 percent of the cash in a family charitable trust. John's comment on this was vintage Crean: "You get an income and you can drive so many cars, wear so many shoes — so you give the rest away." Donna's observation paralleled this sentiment: "What we have, we are supposed to share with others."

Some of the rich as well as some of the not-so-wealthy have made the personal decision to give much of themselves and their wealth to causes and programs they value. They amass wealth, but many of them follow the recommendation of that excellent book, *Die Broke*. At some point many wealthy people recognize that they owe much to the society that nurtured them and guided them down the Giving Path to a point where they actively shifted their priorities and became immersed in a more beneficent stewardship of their wealth. Let me tell you about a few who have chosen the Giving Path.

Gladys Holm who died in 1996 at the age of 86, was known at Children's Memorial Hospital, Chicago, Illinois, as "The Teddy Bear Lady." She was a retired secretary living alone in a modest apartment in Evanston, Illinois, who took pleasure in bringing sick children teddy bears to brighten their spirits; when she died, she left the hospital $18 million to be used for medical research involving diseases of the heart! The teddy bears were her opportunity to visit sick children and find out about their families' financial needs; if a family had no money to pay for their sick child's treatments, Gladys took care of their medical bills. She always did so anonymously.

Miss Holm did not tell the world about her great wealth. She had been the secretary to the founder of American Hospital Supply, Foster McGraw (himself one of America's great philanthropists). She had been given stock options with American Hospital Supply when the company went public in 1951, and her holdings soared in value. Her little secret of giving away teddy bears helped save lives, and her generous donations after her death will impact the lives of thousands of children in years to come.

We may not have millions of dollars to donate, but we can have Miss Holm's spirit of giving and offer a teddy bear to brighten the day of a suffering child. Give what *you* can to make a difference. There is a teddy bear in all of us: It just might be that your teddy bear will be a powerful example to others, young and old. It may be what draws some into the wonderful world of volunteering and philanthropy.

Moving along the Giving Path, we see Ted Turner, an enterprising billionaire (who are few in number). While his business talents are legion, he generated a great deal more attention and praise when he announced his philanthropic plan for his personal wealth.

At fifty-nine, a billionaire, he was full of surprises. As he stepped to the microphone in New York City, the audience knew that he had already amassed a fortune from his twenty-four-hour news network — CNN — and other innovative enterprises; he had captained a winning America's Cup team and had been chosen by *Time* magazine as Man of the Year; he cheered his Atlanta Braves to the World Series; and he had capped off his personal life by marrying a movie star. What new surprise could he possibly spring on the assembly of the United Nations Association, which had gathered to give him an award?

The audience did not know that from December 31, 1996, until the evening of September 18, 1997, his personal net worth had increased from $2.2 billion to $3.2 billion. They also did not know that his surprise announcement would raise a positive call for volunteer philanthropy heard around the world. This billionaire stepped up to the microphone and announced that he was making a $1 billion gift to United Nations programs around the world, giving $100 million a year for a decade. He also issued a challenge: he urged his fellow billionaires and other super-rich individuals to start giving back to the world as volunteers and philanthropists. As only he could say it: "I'm putting every rich person in the world on notice. They're going to be hearing from me about giving money away." Many wealthy individuals have already heard Ted Turner's call and responded. Among those is George Soros, who soon after the Turner announcement pledged $500 million to assist Russia in the retraining of Russian soldiers for successful civilian lives. This was in addition to hundreds of millions of dollars that Soros has already given to Eastern European causes.

Professional athletes receive some of the highest salaries in the world, and yes, many of them do give back. Sports celebrities are famous for signing baseballs or basketballs for auctions at charity fundraisers, making personal appearances at charitable events to raise money, and granting wishes to terminally ill children through such charities as the Make-a-Wish Foundation. Many athletes also make significant contributions to the communities who support their teams by raffling themselves off at public appearances and speaking at schools to encourage children to avoid drugs and finish school.

David Robinson, the center for the San Antonio Spurs basketball team, was selected in 1996 as one of the fifty greatest players in NBA history. He and his wife, Valerie, have pledged what is believed to be the largest single donation by any professional athlete, a $5 million gift to help inner-city youth in San Antonio, Texas. As Robinson proudly commented, "We want to take kids and make them into leaders, and this is going to be a great opportunity!" And major-league baseball players united their charitable efforts in 1996 to form the Players Trust for

Children and raised $1 million by donating at least 2 percent of their licensing income to help start the ongoing trust. The list of voluntary good deeds by professional athletes is endless. Sure, they make a lot of money, but many of them give a lot of money and time back. You might not make as much as they do, but how much of what *you* have are *you* giving back?

Are you interested in the performing arts? If so, then call your local theater or dance company. Are you interested in visual art? Call your local museum or art school. Are you interested in music? Call your local symphony, musical group, or high-school marching band. There is no end to the opportunities for you to give. In New Jersey, a shy philanthropist, Raymond G. Cambers, recently gave $12 million as the lead gift for the New Jersey Performing Arts Center in Newark. After making a fortune several years ago, he retired to spend the rest of his life giving time and money to others.

Henry Kravis, the LBO King is raising millions for inner-city causes in New York. Dave Thomas, founder of Wendy's International, not only gives millions to help poor children (he was one himself), but he gives time to children who need help. Thomas is a role model for children, but he is also a model for rich people who want to return to society some of the benefits they have received.

Americans are also being encouraged to give by Oprah Winfrey, who is generously lending her name and celebrity status to encourage active giving and volunteerism through a national movement she is calling "Oprah's Angel Network." Oprah has used her popular television show to deliver her specific five-point program for volunteer participation around the country: 1) by asking Americans to save their spare change to deposit into the world's largest piggy bank for college scholarships and needy youth; 2) by joining other volunteers with Habitat for Humanity International to build 205 homes in every town that broadcasts *Oprah;* 3) by asking people to work free of charge once a week or once a month by using their job-related skills and talents to help someone in need; 4) by helping at a school to teach a child to read or with other projects; 5) and by creating mini-miracles in the city or community where the Oprah Angel resides.

Many great theater and movie celebrities have taken on a second job — not to build a bigger personal fortune, but to help America's needy. According to Dan Borochoff, president of the Institute of Philanthropy, famous figures can bring in millions of dollars for a charity and also bring it welcomed attention. Comic Relief, the fundraiser hosted by Robin Williams, Whoopi Goldberg, and Billy Crystal, is a tour de force highlighting the best in comedy over the years. This popular trio of comics and their fellow laugh merchants have raised more than $70 million to aid the homeless and needy. The list of generous entertainment stars is a veritable Who's Who. Joan Rivers and Liz Taylor are strong advocates for AIDs causes. Mary Tyler Moore has become the premier spokesperson for Juvenile Diabetes, an affliction she lives with. Actress Shelley Fabares supports education and research for Alzheimer's disease. Jerry Lewis has been a one-man lightning rod for muscular dystrophy research for more than twenty years; his weekend telethons have brought millions of dollars to medical research.

Motives for Giving and Sharing

*He who wishes to secure the good of others
has already secured his own.*
CONFUCIUS

The Independent Sector probed people's motives for giving and contributing to charitable organizations. A national cross-section of households was asked to rate the importance of some key motives for giving. The motives cited most often were:

REASONS FOR GIVING	% RATED VERY IMPORTANT
I was asked to give by someone I know well	25
I'm a volunteer at the organization	25
I was asked by my clergy to give	20
Reading or hearing about a name star	9
Someone came to my door soliciting for a charity	6
Got a letter, asking for a donation	5
Asked at work to give	4

According to these responses, being approached by someone we know well or giving because we volunteer at the facility or organization are the two major motives. Just this last evening, a friend of mine was contacted by a local political figure he knew. In barely two minutes, this candidate presented her platform and asked for a $500 donation; when the donor replied that she would give $250, payment by credit card, the entire transaction took less than two minutes. Amazingly, many organizations need to keep in mind that people will take action (usually favorably) if you present a sound description of your mission and ask them face-to-face to make a donation.

The overwhelming reasons for not donating center around a lack of funds and economic uncertainty. For the most part, people do not give for the following reasons:

REASONS FOR NOT GIVING	% RATED VERY IMPORTANT
I could not afford to give money	46
I'm making less money now compared to last year	26
I lost my job	19
I'm worried about my job	17
I would rather spend my money in other ways	17

Overall, when respondents were asked to contribute money or other property to charitable organizations, some 85 percent of those who were asked complied. Fundraisers and charitable organizations are very attuned to the power of "face-to-face" requests. They know them to be high-energy transactions that are usually successful.

Not all giving is as profound and inspiring as the giving plans of Ted Turner, but there is ever so much we can start and nurture that communicates our loving concern. Rich or poor, we all get opportunities to dream and to involve ourselves in important causes or nonprofit organizations that we feel drawn to. For example, superstar Paul Newman has worked with various food manufacturers and processors to create a top-quality line of food products, including salad dressings and spaghetti sauce. The products became very successful, and Newman decided to give all of his profits to charitable causes. The amount he has given to date has been estimated to exceed $67 million. Even if his gift was only one-half of that amount, it takes great faith and love to be so generous. It is also reassuring to know that he is not waiting until his funeral to make these precious funds available for charity. I thank heaven that what we are seeing in people like Paul Newman is the beginning of a much more compassionate and sensitive awareness of our nation's needy.

In recent years there has been an awesome interest in both acquiring and giving of personal wealth; in some instances the amounts can be mind-boggling. More than 150 contributions of $50 million or more have been given, three of which were for $1 billion each. Bill Gates, the founder of Microsoft, has a personal fortune of more than $40 billion. And some might say that such a sum is downright indecent. True, it's an amazing amount, but he does not intend to have it sit in his oversized vault. He has publicly stated that in a few years he plans to turn his attention away from the world of high tech and devote his life to giving away 95 percent of his personal wealth. Wouldn't it be a wonderful experience if we could join him in his efforts to make this nation a healthier and happier place? There is every indication that the super-rich are not unmindful of their special blessings and unique good fortune. Such wealth needs to be put back "into play" as soon as possible. Bill Gates and Ted Turner and George Soros are charter members of the "Billionaire Club," and their plans regarding the disposition of their wealth is heartwarming. To quote George Bernard Shaw, "When I die I want to be all used up!" What a way to go, having shared it with all the others.

S·I·X

THE ART OF ASKING

On Becoming a Successful Fundraiser

Blessed are the money raisers . . . for in heaven
they shall stand on the right hand of the martyrs.

JOHN R. MOTT

In order for most people to be motivated to give they must first be asked, and asking involves for both professionals and volunteers a knowledge of good fundraising techniques. One of the most important tasks that confront nonprofit charitable organizations is fundraising. Be it the Red Cross or a small shelter for the homeless, they all need the flow of the lifeblood of the nonprofit sector: the money to operate and provide services.

As you may have already concluded, fundraising is a peculiarly difficult assignment for many volunteers. Ever so many staff workers and volunteers have a strong aversion to telephone and in-person solicitation. There are any number of reasons for this resistance; chief among them are:

- "I just hate being rejected."
- "I lose control of my script and get easily confused and nervous when asking for money."
- "I don't meet people easily — cold canvassing especially turns me off."

Even when the fundraisers have a powerful script and read cue cards (eliminating the need to improvise), their limited confidence in their persuasive and presentation skills sabotages them. They seem to mirror the fundraiser's classic lament: "If you think you can't do the fundraising job successfully, you probably can't." Sad to say, in my more than thirty years of professional fundraising, this negative mind-set appears everywhere I have visited or spoken. "I will do anything as long as it isn't fundraising": These are the sentiments of many volunteers.

Fortunately, I have a pretty good remedy for this aversion to raising money. I have always loved fundraising. It has been one of the real joys in my life. Why? Because in truth I do not raise money. I don't dig into people's pockets; I don't get pushy or persistent or obnoxious. All I do is "offer opportunities" for others to give. You see, I have a little secret. I know that if I tell prospective donors that the greatest joy in the world is giving, they will be interested, and I am fearless as an "opportunity offerer." I make it possible for prospects to experience the joy of making the world a better place for others through giving. In their giving to others, they experience the real fulfillment in life which they seek for themselves.

One very important factor to keep in mind is that volunteers will seldom be successful and confident in fundraising until they personally experience the joy of giving money themselves. Once you have been touched by the happiness that comes to you through giving, you will want to share And offer others the same opportunity to give that you have experienced yourself.

Sharing yourself and your reasons for giving is not selling or soliciting. Some prospects are ready to take advantage of the "opportunity" you want to share with them, while others have not yet reached the action stage. Everybody wants to be proud of their compassion and concern for others; if you can stay in touch with your own positive emotions about giving, you need never fear contact with a prospect. Fundraising activities also provide the perfect opportunity to give more information about your cause and sometimes your belief in your mission and what giving does for you can prove to be infectious. You will be a living, breathing example of the joy of giving. I'm not talking about putting on a phony spiritual show or exaggerated presentation — just people-to-people with a humble message, no hard sell, no pushy tactics, just a loving exchange of opportunities.

In my fundraiser training sessions, I focus on the bonds between the fundraiser and the prospects — I emphasize all of the physical, emotional, and spiritual benefits that you are able to offer to the prospective donor. This has made many friends for me. Unlike the common misconception many have about fundraising, people like to be asked, and they admire askers. Are you on the board of a Fortune 500 corporation? I am. How did I get there? I asked the chairman of a Fortune 500 corporation for a million dollars and he gave it. He liked the way I asked him so much that he put me on his board of directors.

Fundraising efforts are actually launched by charities to bring in funds to operate, to construct buildings, or to endow programs. While any donation is appreciated, certain charities and organizations reach out to different demographic segments of the population. For example, one fundraising program may be a mall canvassing to get funds to build or enlarge a shelter for battered women. The donations may average $5 per donor, but some additional information about the shelter shared with mall visitors may give the fundraiser an opportunity to ask for $25. Quite a different fundraising program would involve personal visits to selected potential donors to a museum to ask for gifts in the $5,000 to $25,000 range. Visits can have a dramatic impact on the size of gifts, particularly because the issue becomes close to many people's hearts when they see and touch it. And keep in mind that a large proportion of donors and volunteers only come forward if and when they are asked. They are not lazy or indifferent; they just have not been approached or recruited. I am often asked to summarize successful fundraising in one sentence. The Bible has done it for me already: "Ask and you shall receive."

How efficiently a fundraising program functions is largely influenced by the personal capabilities and characteristics of the fundraising team. One professional fundraiser with years of frontline experience has singled out the following major traits shared by successful fundraisers:

- Strong leadership skills
- Good writing skills
- Ability to work well with volunteers
- Ability to listen to others
- Attention to detail and good management skills
- High self-esteem
- Integrity and honesty
- Sense of humor
- Excellent personal giving habits
- Fearless as an asker

I personally give special attention to the fundraiser's ability to listen to others. It is important to try not to analyze the potential donor's remarks and get caught up in one element of their conversation while missing the comments that may indicate the possibility of a gift. When I am on a fundraising appointment, I first look at the prospect's environment, what has been chosen for display because he or she is proud of the persons or events represented. I comment on the display by asking a "leading question:" "Did you catch that fish? Tell me about it." "Are they your children? Tell me about them." It also gives the fundraiser a natural opportunity to just be friends, with no pressure.

How do you listen once you have asked leading questions? You listen with your eyes, riveting your senses of sight and sound on the prospect — listen for natural opportunities to probe by concentrating on the prospect with your eyes. Keep in mind that if the prospect does make a sizable donation, much of the success belongs to him or her; chances are that you just played the part of enabler and allowed the donor to convince himself or herself while you wisely concentrated on his or her interests and philosophy by simply listening.

I would be remiss if I didn't give you a word of caution. If you are new to fund raising and you think you would like to try it, great! But stay alert to your feelings and how you are coping with resistance. If your intuition says that fundraising just isn't for you, leave it. Ask for an assignment that better suits your feelings and self-esteem as a volunteer. You can make a difference, but only if you are comfortable.

My knowledge of fundraising has been guided by a number of beliefs and principles, one of which is the verity that if you can get a potential donor to make a definitive commitment to a cause, that person will eventually become an above-average contributor. Before you ask for any money, get them involved — let them see the nonprofit operation from the "inside" as a volunteer, not as a shopper "just looking." In my world, major donations always follow a commitment to the cause or organization.

Sometimes, to keep the nonprofit alive and operating, reckless or unwise programs surface and bring into question whether or not the charity or service organization is maintaining mission integrity. Fundraising teams know when they are edging towards questionable tactics or untrue statements about their services or how many received help. If you are a prospective volunteer fundraiser, ask around in the community or among service groups and find out what kind of reputation your nonprofit has. And always remember that this is a people-to-people business: the donor gives money to the person who asks not just to an image. Fundraisers are very often the contact that motivates prospective donors to give. Remember Lawson's Law to guide your fundraising efforts: *People give money to people, and they give most to the person who asks.*

Seven Habits of Successful Fundraisers

I'm sure that some successful fundraisers are just born with special persuasive talents, but my experience says that they are more likely a product of much effort and struggle. As a group, their fundraising efforts seem to parallel the following guidelines, which I call the "Seven Habits of Successful Fundraisers":

1	Successful fundraisers	GIVE	before they ask
2	Successful fundraisers	BELIEVE	in their cause
3	Successful fundraisers	LISTEN	before they talk
4	Successful fundraisers	NEGOTIATE	never intimidate
5	Successful fundraisers	ARE PERSISTENT	not overbearing
6	Successful fundraisers	ARE GRATEFUL	not greedy
7	Successful fundraisers	ARE POSITIVE	not negative

Successful fundraisers are, above all, "Artful Askers" alert and committed to these Seven Habits. As both a professional fundraiser and as a volunteer fundraiser for those nonprofit organizations where I am a board member, I try to practice these habits every day. I hope you will too.

S·E·V·E·N

THE POWERFUL INFLUENCE
OF RELIGION

Like a Rock

*Deeds of giving are equivalent to the entirety
of God's Commandment.*

THE TALMUD

Giving to religious organizations eclipses that to all other nonprofit entities in terms of donations and contributions. Religious instruction is also a powerful influence on the giving patterns and social responsibility felt by many individuals. People who attend religious services are much more active and committed to giving, sharing, and volunteering, (the indicator used to measure the level of religious involvement is the frequency of attendance at services.) According to the most recent study of giving and volunteering, three-quarters of all respondents reported attending religious services sometime during the year; nearly four out of ten attended services nearly every week. Moreover, those who had any attendance during the year reported a much higher rate in household giving (74 percent in 1996) than those who did not attend services at all. According to the Independent Sector, as attendance increases, so does giving.

Volunteer activity is also very heavily influenced by the frequency of attendance at services — almost one half of those who attended religious services in 1996 also did volunteer work, but only one of three who had not attended services performed volunteer work. The average regular religious service goer gives 2.4 percent of his annual income to philanthropic causes, while the non-churchgoer donated only 0.6 percent of their household income. The spiritual connection still appears to be a driving force behind much of the nation's benevolence.

Extended Religious Family

It would seem that religious organizations are expanding their influence and presence in their communities. In many ways local religious organizations have gradually taken on more and more missions and provide more and more services in response to social, economic, spiritual and emotional pressures. As I commented at the beginning of this book, all is not well in Camelot — family ties are tenuous, divorce, disease, and debt race like plagues, causing marital and family problems, health problems, work problems, failures, financial setbacks, loneliness, and despair seem to form an endless river. It is in this troubled river that the churches of America must navigate a passage. In recent years the sharp increase in single parents, divorces and two parents in the workplace has brought a legion of tots to church doors for safe day care, latchkey supervision, and preschool education. These services are popular because they struggle to be ecumenical and the parents trust the religious personnel — it is truly an extended family. Religious instruction, child/parent counseling, and recreation are part of the daily menu at thousands of churches.

Some fifty years ago, religious groups were less challenged; social issues were less diverse; most families had two parents with a mother who stayed at home; divorce and marital problems were apt to be concealed; and the economy was buoyant and full of promise for our returning armed forces — happy days were here again! Against the social tapestry of the year 2000, religious organizations have been pressured to undertake many new tasks and provide numerous new social services for both members of their congregation and for nonmembers who reside nearby. The good pastor, rabbi, or priest is now asked to perform many more duties and to provide many more human services. The pastor's fundamental role as spiritual healer, advisor and teacher must somehow embrace these tasks *in addition* to all of the logistics of the many other social services.

Financial support of religious organizations is a critical issue, and their economic health often depends upon the socioeconomic makeup of their service area and the presence of some loving members with generous deep pockets. At some churches, synagogues, or mosques, the social and religious bonds are very strong and supportive. The challenges are met squarely by the entire congregation, and responsibilities are met with faith and love — they practice what they preach. In their enlarged role as an extended family, religious groups have found that there are great opportunities to demonstrate the Golden Rule and other vital spiritual messages that focus on altruism and religious teachings touch every part of the extended family. Depending upon their lifestyles and needs, some churchgoers may see the church solely as a place of worship and spiritual instruction, but many more give time to some of the church's primary missions or human-services outreach programs. As one pastor proudly proclaimed, "My church is now 85 percent volunteers and 15 percent waiting angels."

The homeless, the mentally troubled, addicts, and the elderly poor are a special challenge. The needy tend to gravitate towards religious organizations because they are often the only institutions that show them any concern or compassion. Volunteer members of religious groups do what they can, putting in billions of volunteer hours to feed, clothe and shelter the indigent, the homeless, and the addicted. For many, helping the community's needy is a compassionate venture, one that federal and local organizations do not always serve effectively or compassionately. And now, amidst all of the other services that religious organizations have been providing to their flocks, there arrives the ubiquitous computer. Since our nation — and to a lesser extent other advanced nations — have become an *information-driven society* just about every conceivable institution now uses computers; while not a particularly spiritual mission for a church, computer literacy is one that can have far-reaching consequences, both emotionally and economically, for members and others the church serves. The computer has become a key element in our economy, and the unemployed and those difficult to place (including the illiterate) are now attending computer classes taught by — you guessed it — church volunteers. Thus, the range of religious volunteer programs and services can be endless and the demands even greater. Take a minute, if you will, to scan the many activities that are offered by the typical religious organization. Considering the limited budgets and staff of churches, synagogues, and mosques, and the even greater poverty of some of the members — it's a miracle that so much positive progress is being made.

Some of the Services and Programs Provided by Today's Religious Groups:

- Religious worship
- Religious instruction
- Christenings/marriage ceremonies
- Funeral services
- Pastoral/spiritual counseling
- Choir, music
- Religious theater and allied arts
- Hospital visitations with sick and the infirm; hospice assistance
- Job counseling/guidance for teens
- Marital counseling
- Housing advice/legal assistance to church members
- Meals for senior citizens
- Recreation for elderly (bingo, lectures, etc.)
- Young adult recreation (movies, games, dancing, music)
- Summer camp youth clubs
- Day care kindergarten services
- Latchkey supervision
- Computer orientation for children
- Physical training (exercise classes) for young adults and children
- Job counseling and placement for adults
- Training of volunteers for specific service programs

- Facilities for self-help and recovery groups such as single parents, AA, ALANON, ACOA, OA, etc.
- Food, shelter, counseling, clothing for the homeless
- Basic language classes and education for immigrants
- Thrift shops for special rummage sales (fundraising)
- Training for meal delivery to shut-ins
- Transportation to medical facilities for the infirm
- Holiday meals for needy families and individuals
- Weekly food supplement for the needy
- Caregiving for the infirm

With all of these service programs in operation, churchgoers get to develop friendships, and a special bonding takes place. At the church, synagogue, or mosque people develop associations and friendships that are long lasting. Some come to seek assistance, others offer to serve and volunteer. Out of the controlled chaos of an active and involved church can come a special acceptance and belonging. Finally, consider all of these activities and services in the light of the high mobility of church members who change careers, change partners, change homes, and change cities. Changes require adjustments for everyone. Newcomers are welcomed, departure is sweet sorrow, and the church remains the foundation of the community — *solid as a rock.*

Some Clouds of Concern

Many religious volunteer programs are not without their critics. Some of the concern involves the nature of the programs. Do they have a solid mission and goals statement that guide the organization's efforts? Can the religious organization measure its results and effectiveness? There is also concern about focused and organized vs. informal religious programs.

U.S. News and World Report published a challenging feature article entitled (April 28, 1997) "Is Volunteering a Waste of Time?" They posed the question "Do do-gooders do much good?" The reporters' major criticism centered around the ability of volunteer programs to solve core problems. Perhaps these critics should observe how, right now, federal and state governments are trying to redistribute major social-welfare programs to the level and to the extent possible recruit nonprofit and religious volunteers to handle many of the non-professional needs. Most religious volunteers are not equipped, prepared, or qualified to replace a professional caseworker, counselor, or accredited social worker, but in many cases they can get the job done.

One critic inquired, "What about these 93 million volunteers, who have reported that they labored 20 billion hours in 1996 — that works out to 218 hours per person, per year!" He claimed that the productivity calculations need to be adjusted because some 25 percent of volunteer hours were used for informal work such as baby-sitting or baking cookies. The *U.S. News and World Report* writers claimed that only 8.4 percent of the 93 million volunteers work directly on essential human services, a category that involves families in crisis, the homeless, counseling, and

Red Cross disaster relief. Overall, less than 4 percent of volunteers serve as tutors, and just 1.2 percent as mentors or drug counselors.

The director of the Institute for Policy Studies at Johns Hopkins claims that only about 7 to 15 percent of volunteering done through religious organizations goes beyond the religious groups' walls to the surrounding community. Many religious volunteers landscape the grounds of their worship place, repair facilities, and cook for various in-house parties, celebrations, and visitations.

For many years, conservative politicians have pushed for greater support from religious organizations to take on more of the nation's social-welfare burden. For me, part of the issue centers on responsibility (who should do what?) and resources (who pays for the training, the facilities, the leadership, the recruiting, and the administrative duties?). It will take more than one 1997 Presidential Summit Meeting for America's Future to develop the essentials of a broad scale program that is quasi-governmental, but with General Colin Powell's help and that of thousands of churches, synagogues, mosques, corporations, and other organizations, it can be done.

As we look at the present situation in this country, much focus is placed on the nature of the social-welfare needs that are not currently being adequately delivered, such as illiteracy programs, mentoring of youth in trouble, help for drug abusers, help for dysfunctional families, foster parenting, assistance to battered women, prevention of child abuse, help for families in distress, the aid to homeless, as well as adequate medical care for the many physical and emotional problems of the aged.

I'm sure that there under certain crisis situations religious groups will adequately meet the emerging needs of the suffering and troubled. But religious volunteers usually place God, family, and their religious group in that order, and *then* expand to helping others. One pressing issue, simply stated, is: Can you depend upon church volunteers to fill the gaps left by state and national government's failures and cutbacks in welfare and other programs for the needy?

If we view religious volunteerism in the terms of a business operation, then it is considered by some to be a very inefficient one. Most of the more demanding and complicated services rendered to those in need are administered by government staff workers who have professional credentials. At this juncture, some claim that amazingly little is known about which religious group's volunteer programs really work well and which are marginal. I have, however, seen many great results: Habitat for Humanity International is a popular religion-oriented volunteer service that is usually oversubscribed every week; it performs an amazing service, for simple decent places to live are built by volunteers for people living in substandard housing around the world. And this is not a hand-out, for the people who get the houses must also volunteer to help build their own homes and those for their neighbors, and they must also be willing and able to pay for their house through an interest-free mortgage.

People do want to volunteer at their churches, synagogues or mosques and make a difference, but many have demanding work schedules. Some talented individuals often serve only one day a year — with no free time they are not able to be trained for a more useful and complicated intervention. One teaching expert reported that mentoring and tutoring require considerable committed time and high levels of patience and consistency; to be effective, volunteers must put in thirty to sixty minutes per session, two or three days a week. Below this hourly duration, he says, "You are not really helping. Tutoring is very demanding."

We can see that measuring the value and efficiency of religious volunteer programs is difficult. Moreover, religious volunteers are, as a rule, not efficiency or cost-control specialists; they don't ordinarily think in those terms, and it would seem that they hear a different drummer, one who sounds compassion and encouragement , not economic efficiency.

I firmly believe that religious volunteers can be of service in ways that are important to our nation. They can certainly organize and staff many new outreach services, but we need to keep firmly in mind that they are not foot soldiers in the state and federal social-service militias. They are soldiers of a different Army — they serve God, not a state. This at one and the same time makes religious volunteerism a powerful force for good, while at the same time exposing it to many inherent weaknesses.

E·I·G·H·T

GETTING INVOLVED

Matching Your Talents to the Opportunities

*Each citizen should plan his part in the community
according to his individual gifts.*

PLATO

You personally can make a difference. Your community needs your gifts of money, but it also needs your time and your special skills. Many people take the first opportunity that comes along to volunteer, but it makes more sense to work at what you do best. If you do, you will be happier, and you will make more of an impact.

The kind of organization you support is important. Each of us is unique, so different causes will appeal to different people, and since there are more than 600,000 active nonprofit organizations in America to choose from, there is bound to be one for you. If one cause doesn't strike a responsive emotional chord, if you don't feel some natural pull, then pass it by. You may feel you ought to volunteer for a given cause simply because you were asked to, but this sort of half-hearted commitment may dilute your time and resources and lead you to give less to an activity that really means a lot to you. Extra energy and emotional dividends will come from a solid commitment to a cause you believe in.

Most people give at least some of their time and money to their own religious institution, and if you are looking for an opportunity to volunteer, this would be a good place to start. Most denominations provide a wealth of services to many kinds of people with many needs. Yours might have local programs to feed or shelter the homeless, aid international famine relief, offer legal assistance to the poor or support for the arts, work to improve the environment, care for preschool children, or provide meals and activities for the elderly, and perhaps many, many more. You can easily find out about which programs your denomination offers by getting in touch with its local or regional offices. Such work often leads to positions of responsibility and leadership.

There usually isn't one single clearinghouse in a community for people interested in volunteer work, so a person who wants to volunteer needs to be inquisitive and persistent. The United Way is another good place to begin in your community; there you can find out about local service opportunities in its participating organizations.

What skills do you have? Probably more than you think. Take a minute and write down what you feel you do best. Your goal is to be comfortable and satisfied with your volunteer work and to have a sense of mastery over your task, even if it's as simple as stuffing envelopes. When people know they can do a job, they are less likely to feel threatened or disheartened. As you make this inventory, assess your skills in:

- Teaching and instructing
- Persuasion and sales; fundraising
- Administration and clerical work
- Counseling and guidance
- Socializing and entertaining

- Analysis and writing
- Creative and artistic work
- Construction, repair, and crafts
- Logistics and organization
- Public speaking and advocacy
- Physical assistance and caretaking

After all, if you have a clear idea of what you can do and enjoy doing, the choice you make is more likely to be suited to your skills and interests. If you have poor organizational skills, let someone else organize the charity dance. If you have flat feet or knee trouble, don't volunteer as a sidewalk Santa. But if you are good at balancing a checkbook, you might enjoy doing the accounting for a charity marathon. If you are good at listening and hugging, consider volunteering to visit a nursing home weekly.

Most people have pretty good instincts about what activities fit their talents and interests. When a poor possibility is presented to you, some emotional response probably your blood pressure — will signal if it's a poor fit. Listen to these internal signals and take on only the tasks that feel right. If one doesn't seem comfortable or "doable," say no and wait for the next opportunity.

Many people may feel that the four or five hours they can give each week are not worth the self-analysis and detailed planning I am recommending, but I believe that such efforts will make your volunteer time and giving much, much more pleasurable and effective. Commitment and a good match are the beginning of good service. You can take control of your own volunteer time and turn it into an adventure. There's no better time to start than now.

Getting Started, Doing More — A New Approach

Do all the good you can,
By all means you can,
In all the ways you can,
In all the places you can,
At all the times you can,
To all the people you can,
As long as you ever can.

JOHN WESLEY

Most Americans give both money and time to others. The Independent Sector says that 49 percent of adults volunteer time each year, on average four hours a week. The typical American household donates about $700 a year to charity, and that figure includes *all households* (those that gave and those that didn't). I am sure that most Americans have volunteered or given money at some point in life, often with great satisfaction.

However, sometimes the experience of giving or volunteering is tedious or even unpleasant. As one disgruntled volunteer said to me, "What's the use in complaining? My intentions were good." One especially energetic volunteer told me about her troubles in trying to work with orphanage babies. She applied at her local Foundling home and had her background checked, spent four nights in class learning to care for the infants, and only then was told there were no volunteer openings for a year. One dedicated volunteer told me how he doggedly raised money even though he hated making cold canvass calls.

Incidents like these can wound the spirit. People don't say much about them because they mistakenly believe that giving and volunteering are supposed to be unpleasant or sacrificial. The needy recipients benefit, to be sure, but for the volunteer it is just work, "giving up" something in order to be of service. Although this is a fairly common attitude, it is dead wrong. Acts of giving and sharing need not be unpleasant.

Many donors and volunteers in philanthropic work are miscast. We often commit ourselves to service before considering whether or not the job fits us; out of a sense of duty we show up and work at tasks we dislike. I don't claim that every moment of volunteer activity should be a peak experience, but there are steps you can take to choose the right area of service for you and improve your experience of volunteer work.

The first step is to find out who you are and how you feel about service. Ask yourself these questions:

- How well do you get along with people?

- Do you work well in cooperative efforts with demanding people? In tense situations?

- Do you prefer structured or unstructured work?

- Do you like selling, soliciting, or negotiating? Are you comfortable asking people for support, money, or assistance?

- Do you need frequent or immediate feedback, or do you work well with little or no recognition?

- Do you work best when you primarily direct your own efforts, or when others are in charge?

- Do you enjoy doing work you know you can do, or do you enjoy stretching your limits?

- Are you drawn to difficult or seemingly impossible causes?

- What projects do you remember that you loved, where you "lost yourself?"
- List ten activities you know or think you would enjoy.

Be honest with yourself, and pick volunteer work that fits you. Believe me, it's out there. I think that most unhappiness among volunteers comes from taking on work that doesn't fit their character or emotional needs: If you don't like asking strangers for money, don't do it; there are many, many other ways to help. It's important to know or sense what fits you. Dr. Hans Selye says, "Much of the trouble people have comes from their trying to be something they are not."

When you give or volunteer it's important to enjoy the experience, not necessarily every moment but for many of the moments. The quality of your volunteer experiences will determine the physical, psychological, and spiritual benefits you receive from sharing. If you are at odds with your assignment or experiencing personality clashes, all you'll receive from your giving efforts will be more stress, not harmony and well-being.

It's easy to see how stressful situations can arise. When people admire the work of an organization, they gladly volunteer. Many will say, in effect, "I'll do whatever I'm asked. So many people volunteer, you have to take what they give you." Others will assume they don't have the right to ask for a special assignment lest they be labeled demanding or difficult.

Yet active pursuit of the right kind of work for you is the only approach that makes sense. You can't experience the rewards of giving if you're trapped in a boring, irritating, or unsatisfying assignment. If it seemed right at first but then turned wrong for you, ease your way out of it. It's essential that you gain some satisfaction and joy from your volunteer time.

Negative voices about volunteering are strong: "Get real, most volunteer work is just plain boring." "The organization I support doesn't have interesting jobs." "If you think you can enjoy this, you're living in a dream world!"

If you are hearing these voices, I suggest two ways to change your experience:

- Look for a cause where your needs are more likely to be met — there are thousands. Find out about other organizations and their needs and projects.

- Stay with your current cause, but create an assignment for yourself that fits you. Find a change of pace.

The benefits that can come from supporting a cause you believe in are extraordinary, but you won't experience them unless you take your own needs into account and aim for enjoyable experiences. You can maximize your opportunities if you keep in mind Dr. Csikszentmihalyi's conditions for peak experiences. Pick a task . . .

- that you are capable of doing.
- that has clear goals and structure.
- that provides immediate feedback.
- where you can exercise some control over circumstances.
- where involvement becomes effortless and you feel absorbed, where your self-consciousness disappears.
- where time passes quickly and pleasurably.

Greater satisfaction is also possible when giving money. Investigate the cause you are interested in — call the people in charge. Visit them. Find out more about their needs. Earmark your funds for a particular project and follow its progress. Get to know other staff and volunteers in the organization. Find out about other needs; perhaps you have special contacts or resources they can use. When you become personally involved in your giving, you can change an arms-length approach to an arms-around approach.

Barriers to Involvement

It is one of the most beautiful compensations of this life that no man can sincerely try to help another without helping himself.
RALPH WALDO EMERSON

People offer many reasons for not becoming involved in service and giving, in particular shyness, lack of time, or infirmity. These reasons are sometimes real, sometimes excuses. People also are more apt to wait, to hesitate until they are formally asked to help. There are many people who will happily serve if they are just asked in a direct, perhaps flattering, way. Many people, especially busy young professionals, schedule their lives so that there is hardly an unfilled moment in the day. For older people, physical maladies, illness, and limited energy are real problems. Women with families, especially working mothers, have so many demands on their time that they could use a twenty-eight-hour day just to take care of the work they already have; lack of spare time (and energy) put a real limit on what they can offer.

But there are ways to make opportunities for service in a busy life. Look at your schedule and put your current commitments to a couple of simple tests: give yourself a "Value Scale Review." What you're trying to do is free up a few hours a week for volunteer service.

First, let the roaring sound of words like "impossible," "out of the question," and "you must be crazy" die away. You need to have an open mind to explore new alternatives.

Next, list the major blocks of time in your typical workday and days off — what you have to do and what you can change; your days off will probably have more flexible time. Give each activity — work, housework, recreation, exercise, sleep, social events — a value rating from 1 to 5, with 5 being most valuable. Among the 1, 2, or 3 ratings is a possible opportunity for volunteer time. Choose an activity you can most easily change.

Third, select a type of service that interests you. Ignore for the moment the specifics and concentrate on the ideal type for you. Give that service a value rating of 4 and compare it to the activity you selected as easiest to replace. Since much of our workaday life is repetitive, this block of "spare" time will likely be pretty consistent from week to week. After reflection, you might find that you do have a regular time for volunteer service after all.

A simpler approach is the Active/Passive test: watching TV is passive, feeding the children is active. Your passive activities are more easily available for volunteer service time, but even priority activities can be subordinated — maybe the children, if they are old enough, can prepare one meal a week themselves, freeing you up for a few hours.

Most people would gladly give many hours to save a dying child without worrying too much about the displacement of other things in their lives, but most causes don't have this kind of urgency and so they seem less important. And sometimes we really do need private and family time to stay sane, or an extra job to pull us through financially. Illness and infirmity are real. Still, some of our time can be rearranged.

Let's look at some of the thoughts people have which are barriers to involvement:

"I Don't Have Any Special Talents"

This is so often heard and so seldom true. Spending recreational time with older people or helping blind children require compassion and sensitivity. Most volunteer work is easily learned. Think first of the type of service that interests you, and you are sure to find tasks you can already do. Candace Lightner, who founded Mothers Against Drunk Driving (MADD) and is a member of the Lawson Associates team, says she began the organization without any knowledge at all of how to do it — she just did what needed to be done as it came up and learned the ropes as the movement grew.

"I'm Shy and Have Trouble Meeting People"

Deep down, many of us are shy. Shyness is natural and very human. So are spontaneous gratitude, acceptance, and appreciation among volunteers and those we help. There is apt to be a real sense of community and love among volunteers which will embrace you once you take the plunge. Your shyness will diminish if you face your fears, and the

world of service is a receptive place. When you help someone in need, your shyness often just fades away.

"I'm a Person with Only Limited Resources"

Most people don't have much money to spare: Some people
pledge an amount and then get a small part-time job or do
craft work to meet their pledge. Teenagers do neighborhood
chores and give what they earn. Theater groups stage plays
and donate the proceeds. Your resources are limited only by
your imagination. To paraphrase the Bible, where your
commitment is, there will your heart be also.

"There Is No Particular Cause That Interests Me"

Strangely, people sometimes feel this way because they
aren't involved enough. If you only give occasional effort or
stay on the sidelines of a group, you won't get a solid feel
for service — you need to come closer to the fire and feel
the warmth. Grassroots activity is sometimes the answer. I
know a man who was on the board of an overseas relief
agency. He found the board meetings dull, dry, and boring,
so he left his prestigious post and began serving as an
unpaid sales representative promoting the crafts of the foreign communities served by the agency. The simple sales
transaction provided him with a more direct sense of participation and much more personal satisfaction.

"My Charity Begins at Home"

This usually means that our family needs all that we can give
and do; sometimes it is just a humorous admission that
finances are tight. And service *should* begin at home. The

first place to give our energy and love is to those we love the most, and sometimes our family has urgent needs that we simply must address. But outside service can also soften our hearts and lead us to greater sensitivity. We can return home with a renewed love for our families which can help transform a troubled home into a place of warmth and mutual respect. Once your heart has expanded to include others, your own immediate family will also receive your renewed compassion and giving. Dr. Tessa Warschaw in her book *Rich is Better* says, "I have met many . . . successful men and women but none of them have been truly filled up with anything but their relationships, the love that they give. I have never met anyone with money but with no generosity from the heart who has been happy." Remember: Volunteering and sharing are biologic imperatives!

Pacing Yourself — Easy Does It

Seek always to do some good somewhere.
You must give some time to your fellow man, for remember,
you don't live in a world all your own.
ALBERT SCHWEITZER

Another reason many volunteers and benefactors are not satisfied in their giving is that they overextend themselves. While devoting yourself to a cause may be admirable, it can also be self-defeating. Too often we think that what is worth doing is worth overdoing. This may be good for the organization you've chosen, but it isn't good for you. Why? Because driving yourself beyond a sensible limit can lead to disillusionment, resentment, and burnout. I have seen this happen again and again — a person will set out with great optimism, promise more than can be delivered, and then, feeling trapped, push to the limit. The resulting stress always leads to setbacks and dissatisfaction.

Every volunteer should carry a card with five small phrases on it:

- Don't overextend yourself physically.

- Don't overpromise.

- Don't try to do it all alone.

- Don't overreact.

- Do find time to enjoy your work.

Too many people drop out as volunteers because they don't know how to pace themselves. One bad experience can lead to a negative attitude toward volunteerism that can last for a lifetime. The best counsel I know is, "Take small bites." Start slow, be aware of your energy level, and take your time.

Try to see volunteering as an opportunity to find enjoyment and pleasure through sharing. By helping others you enhance your self-image and match your skills to real needs that otherwise might not be met; if these elements are missing, reconsider your commitment. Don't be a martyr. Giving until you drop can only lead to frustration, certainly not to a dynamic, fulfilled life. Slow down, enjoy the journey, and let the experience of sharing gradually fill your life with joy.

Of course, reality always turns out differently than we imagine when we enlist in our chosen cause, and even when our volunteer work is going well, our family and career often demand our attention. When this happens, protect yourself. Back away from your volunteer work until you meet your more basic commitments. It is absolutely appropriate to step back when family or work crises arise, just as it's sensible to step back from an unsatisfactory volunteer task, and there is no loss of personal integrity in such a move. Your goal is both to advance the cause you believe in and to enhance your life. You cannot do either if you are over committed.

Volunteers who serve for many years learn to moderate their efforts. They find opportunities that match their talents. They seek out the tasks that seem sweetest to them, take their time, become comfortable with their assignments, and then do the best they can, and they and their cause both benefit.

Most volunteer, fundraising, and advocacy activities require teamwork, and seldom do two people approach the same project in the same way; some cooperate easily, while others challenge authority. There is always some friction in the volunteer ranks, and I am convinced that this energy helps the total effort, but acceptance of others, tolerance, and patience always enrich the experience. The lack of these qualities can sabotage a project and make the work unpleasant for all. If you find yourself in this kind of situation, again, the best thing to do might be to look for a volunteer task more suited to your needs.

People can be intensely loyal and have strong emotional ties to their causes and the institutions that promote them. For some, their charitable organization is almost an extended family. Their respect and dedication to the organization's goals are unswerving even through hard times. For others, commitments that were once fresh can become burdensome drudgery; these people often stay involved out of pride or closeness to a cause they once held dear. However, people change, and so do their energies and circumstances. If you feel restless, stale, unhappy with difficult leadership, look for a new challenge. Start first within the organization, but if you don't find it there, bring your involvement to closure with grace and thanks for what you have received, and look elsewhere.

Once they have gotten into the swing of volunteering, most people find a number of organizations that they admire and wish to help. A new kind of service can be reinvigorating and exciting — change and challenge keep all of us flexible and involved. This is not desertion, but rather a celebration of your healthy respect for the quality of your own life.

It is important that you find satisfaction and real meaning in your volunteer efforts and giving. They are the key to finding the rewards of philanthropy. Try to follow the advice of the late Leo Buscaglia in his book *Loving Each Other:* "Joy, humor, laughter — all are wonderful, easily accessible tools for bringing comfort . . . . When we feel joyful, euphoric, happy, we are more open to life, more capable of seeing things clearly and handling daily tensions."

Enlisting the Entire Family

*It is a rare and a high privilege to be in a position
to help people understand the difference that they can make
not only in their own lives but in the lives of others
by simple giving of themselves.*
HELEN BOOSALIS

Each volunteer, each donor, each single advocate is a valuable resource, possessing extraordinary powers. Becoming a giver can lead to greater personal harmony and also to greater involvement on the part of your family: By enlisting them in your sharing, you double, triple, or quadruple your contribution to the cause you value.

Perhaps the most successful effort in the history of Religion in American Life was the "Invite a Friend" campaign, which sought to motivate more Americans to attend religious services. For every successful formal solicitation of wealth from an affluent benefactor or foundation, there are tens of thousands of effective requests from friends and relatives. The great philanthropic work of America is built on local person-to-person effort, and every donor and every volunteer counts. A committed volunteer can motivate family and friends and thus widen the circle of the cause he cares about and expand the benefits of sharing. I have often seen entire families work together for a cause, particularly at religious events; I am sure this is tied to lessons learned during religious training. The religious cause benefits mightily from this kind of wholesome response, and families grow in solidarity as well.

When you are considering giving to or joining a cause, why not consult the whole family? Deciding together what to support can have a wonderful effect on family harmony. Working on a cause by parents and children together is a wonderful form of family communion, creating a closer bond of love. Collective ties like this are healing, especially in a society where so many factors weaken family relationships. Truly, the family that gives together grows together.

Sharing the experience of giving is also a way to show children the value of respect and love for others. What better model can a child have than parents who make philanthropy an important part of their lives? A parent who actively works for important values introduces children to a world where they can make a difference and experience the friendship and gratitude of others. A parent's selfless service helps children understand the value of service for others and gives reality to the biblical injunction, "It is better to give than to receive."

Family volunteering also helps children build a positive sense of self as they grow. Young children are highly impressionable and learning much from the world around them. What their parents do never goes unnoticed and seldom goes unimitated. Teaching children generosity of spirit by including them in family philanthropy can have far-reaching positive effects on a child's character, setting them up for a richer and more harmonious life.

By including your children in your giving, you are guiding them to a second path of knowledge that can teach them what formal education cannot. The path of sharing and giving is a path of wisdom, compassion, and involvement with others. As you prepare them for college, career, and a family, give them the gift of giving — it will help them reach a state of well-being that comes from a love of others combined with a proper love of self.

There is a tender trap in this recommendation. The best teaching for children is doing. If you include your children from their earliest ages in your acts of sharing, they will learn the lessons of compassion, cooperation, and dedication to good causes, and working together with them will bind your hearts together.

For two specific groups of family members, the act of sharing is critical. For the very young, learning to be compassionate, sharing, and responsible is essential to their becoming healthy and joyful adults. For the elderly, sharing helps develop a stronger life force, decreases depression and lethargy, and banishes loneliness. Pastoral, medical, and counseling experts all advise older people that sharing their time with others helps avoid isolation and generates self-esteem and respect.

So enlist your family in your sharing. You will be giving them gifts of incalculable value.

N·I·N·E

ALL AGES CAN GIVE

Early Lessons

The heart of the giver makes the gift dear and precious.
MARTIN LUTHER

Modern medical and social scientists agree that a person's patterns of generosity are formed during the first four or five years of life. The parents' example is especially important in determining whether or not a child becomes a person who shares easily. According to Dr. Lee Salk, the way parents and other close relatives behave, what they teach, and how they treat others all set the stage for a child's life as a giving person.

My years of work with religious, academic, cultural, and social welfare groups have given me some insight into what helps people grow into healthy, compassionate adults. I would stress these core experiences of childhood development:

- Early observations and training are critical influences on patterns of giving.

- Parents should provide a variety of giving activities for their children. By doing so they contribute mightily to their children's chances of becoming sensitive and giving adults.

- Small children are naturally self-centered. It is up to parents to introduce the child to a give-and-share lifestyle.

- By the age of three, children understand that other people are different and can begin to identify and empathize with the complex emotions of others.

- Money and how it is valued are important in early child-hood development. When families are insecure about money, that insecurity persists in the child, who as an adult will often develop an obsession with making large sums of money.

- Both word and example are important in teaching children to be generous and caring. If parents verbally encourage sharing but act selfishly, the child will be confused. How can a child learn about sharing hands and an open heart from miserly, withholding parents?

- Sharing is best taught in a child's own terms: "Helping another person makes you happy."

- Parents should encourage small children to act on their own impulses to share. These first spontaneous acts of charity give form and meaning to the child's own experience.

When I was very young I remember my father suggesting that I share my candy, toys, and a few pennies. His approval and praise made me glow with pride and gave me a positive attitude toward giving. I see now that my father was helping me form an image of myself as a sharing person.

A daughter of the Rockefellers told a gathering on National Philanthropy Day in New York City that her father gave her an allowance of fifteen cents a week. He had her make up three boxes: "mine," "savings," and "others." Each week she put one nickel in each box. At Christmastime, she and her father emptied the "others" box and counted it. After much discussion with her father she selected a charity, went to the bank with her father, got a cashier's check for the amount in the box, and mailed it to the charity. She proudly proclaimed that she still followed her father's principle of "one-third to charity."

Giving, sharing, and volunteering involve a complex set of value judgments and motives. Our willingness to help others doesn't spring from a genetic matrix alone. Some recent studies of the roots of childhood sharing and compassion prove to be revealing: Young children cannot easily express their own motives, but two- and three-year-old children can be seen in these studies to share spontaneously with each other. Unfortunately, these children have not yet been tracked (as they grow up) to see if they develop altruistic personalities, but I think it is reasonable to conclude that early givers are lifetime givers. Early misers are lifetime misers except for Scrooge, who is the confused product of Dickens's imagination.

I recently saw a three-year-old child of a friend of mine observe two seven-year-old children eat some candy. The two older children saw the three-year-old staring at them and offered him some of their candy. The three-year-old's immediate response was to offer them some of the potato chips he was eating from a bag held by his father. The whole incident was quite spontaneous and told me a lot about the future character of all three children. Add one fact to this scene and you see how children can teach us: the older children were African-American and the three-year-old was white.

Dr. Bruce Baldwin, a behaviorist, suggests that parents should consider the following ways to teach social responsibility:

- Discuss the values and benefits of sharing and participation with your children. As they grow in understanding, introduce more and more information about these good values.

- Teach your children to help in community and church projects.

- Don't insulate your children from the harsher realities of life. Visit missions, hospitals, homes for the elderly, and poor neighborhoods together to see firsthand the need for sharing.

- Teach your children how to give part of their allowance to a cause that appeals to them.

Too often we give double messages to our young people. On the one hand we encourage them to make money, to be the best, win it all, take charge, work hard, never give up on the American Dream; on the other hand we try to instill in them a sense of responsibility to others and a sharing heart. It seems that today's young adult considers sharing and giving of secondary importance during the climb to personal success. Even sadder is the fact that many people equate empathy for others with weakness.

Our society isn't perfect and never will be, but it would improve if we were to put less emphasis on "making it" and "getting my share of the pie." I don't hear much about "giving my share of the pie." Many see acts of generosity as something to postpone until the big slice of the pie has been won, and until then most energy, effort, and concern stay focused on the race for material success. Some upwardly mobile young Americans seem to worship power, position, and money. It's not the race I mind so much as their single-minded devotion to it, their lack of balance, and the limited energy and resources they have left for community sharing.

Eventually many who work hard to achieve the material dream will pass on their concentrated wealth to their children. Children are great mimics who readily absorb and reflect their parents' behavior, and this driven existence is powerfully attractive. If just 5 percent of this energy could be harnessed to help resolve social and educational problems, it would have a tremendous impact, and these people would begin to discover their capacity for compassionate and empathetic community leadership.

Recently, according to a *New York Times* story, a group of seven-year-olds in Trumbull, Connecticut, were told about the plight of homeless children. The results were astounding and yet they were, for children around the world, quite ordinary: Elizabeth gave $1 from her savings earmarked for a Samantha doll and a present for her brother. Guy Lev gave eighty cents he had been saving for a new Nintendo magazine. His only comment? "People are more important than magazines." Caroline Tanski gave the $10 her grandmother had given her for her eighth birthday. In ten days these and other children in their school collected $468.59 for the homeless. What a lesson in giving for all of us.

America's young people are within the force fields of the electronic media, advertisers, and schools. These institutions do contribute to their formation of generosity. Advertisers especially can show children giving and sharing while the product is being promoted, and children's television shows and books themes of generosity and compassion can be produced. Religious organizations and groups like the Boy Scouts, the Girl Scouts, Boys and Girls Clubs, 4H Clubs, YMCA/YWCA, and other groups for young people have great opportunities to act as mentors and teach a life based on sharing. But the greatest opportunity is right at home, with your own children — now!

Sweet Bird of Youth

People can be divided into three groups:
those who make things happen,
those who watch things happen,
and those who wonder what happened.

NICHOLAS MURRAY BUTLER

A look at the American media's projected image of teenagers shows them to be selfish, self-centered, and self-indulgent. In the mind of the media, our youth crowd into malls to hang out and occasionally shop, spend idle hours watching television and movies, and are fascinated by drugs, sex, and self-destruction.

This picture is not the only one. Teenagers today have a more active social conscience than in any previous generation. Their concern for others is obvious and easily tapped. Today's teenagers are surprisingly dependable, reliable and generous with both their time and their money. A 1995 survey by the Independent Sector found that 53 percent of American teenagers volunteered their time to help others. Actually, more "selfish" teenagers gave of their time that year than adults, only 48 percent of whom volunteered. The widespread belief that teenagers are driven only by their own needs is simply not true.

Teenagers also gave generously. In 1995 half of all American teenagers contributed to charity. The average annual teenage gift that year was $46. This may not seem like much, but teenagers frequently have very little spending money. The total dollar amount that year was close to one quarter of a billion dollars, a large splash in anyone's bucket.

Teenagers in 1989 averaged almost four hours of volunteer time each week, and more than one fourth of them gave five hours or more. They provided a total of 1.6 billion hours of volunteer time. The monetary value of their volunteer hours, when calculated by the minimum wage, is about $5.9 billion. Girls were more active with their time than boys (65 percent of teenage girls volunteered versus 51 percent of the boys), but we should remember that teenage boys are more often employed than girls.

Almost three-quarters of teenage volunteerism takes place through organized programs and charities or involves helping the elderly. It is not uncommon to see fourteen-year and fifteen-year-olds helping feed the homeless at shelters and soup kitchens: Harvey Mandel of the St. Vincent de Paul Joan Kroc Center in San Diego reports that about twenty teenagers volunteer there each week. Students from Point Loma High School served Thanksgiving dinner at the Center recently to more than a thousand street people.

Young people today are not passive observers of society's ills but active forces in shaping the national social conscience. Although teenagers sometimes feel ignored by the adult world, their concerns about peace, the environment, social equality for minorities, along with their compassion for the homeless, make an important contribution to the political and moral dialogue of the nation.

Some other findings about teenagers' generosity:

- Ninety percent of teenagers lent a hand when they were asked. This is hardly selfish resistance. However, young people are usually shy and respond best when they are asked to help. Only one in four volunteered without being asked.

- Forty-eight percent were recruited by friends, twenty-six percent by teachers or school officials, twenty percent by relatives. Family, friends, and school are clearly the forces that move young people to volunteer action.

- Seventy-three percent of teenagers who regularly attend religious services also volunteer, while only thirty-four percent of those who did not attend volunteered. Religion is another powerful motivator for young people.

- Two-thirds of students in schools that have volunteer programs said they gave some of their time.

Teenagers affirm that the principal reasons for volunteering are a desire to be useful to others, enjoyment of the work, the need to do something good with their free time, and a desire to learn and get experience.

Many benefits come to teenagers when they volunteer: They become part of community-wide efforts. Since they put in as much effort as adults, they are treated as equals and experience the world as peers of adults. Their work earns them real gratitude and acceptance, which usually leads to greater self-esteem. They learn about the benefits of giving and sharing. They become part of the give-and-take team effort. And most of all, they see that they have the power to make a difference somewhere in the world.

It is vital that young people be encouraged in their volunteer work. It helps them develop a social conscience and helps form the next generation of leaders for society. Volunteering also helps them experience firsthand the physical, emotional, and spiritual benefits of volunteer involvement.

There are some concrete actions you can take to promote volunteer activity among teenagers:

- Find out what courses and programs involving community volunteer work are offered by the local schools.

- Work with local volunteer agencies and religious organizations to develop ways to tap the special talents and energy of young people.

- Write articles for local newspapers highlighting youth volunteerism. (You might be surprised to find yourself published.)

- Help the media publicize opportunities for young people to volunteer. Suggest to local radio, television, and cable stations that they feature teens working as volunteers, and help develop stories focused on teen volunteers.

- Work with local businesses to establish and publicize scholarships for teen volunteers.

- Prepare a weekly or monthly list of teen volunteer opportunities and distribute it wherever young people congregate — schools, youth clubs, scout organizations, churches, and synagogues.

- Most importantly, talk to your own teenagers about volunteering, follow their progress in what they choose to do, praise their work, and make it an important part of your family conversation. Your increased respect for your teenagers will pay you untold benefits in your family life.

By helping support teenage volunteerism, you can have a powerful effect on your community and its young people. Through your efforts, hundreds of young people may pitch in to help others and, by helping others, help themselves.

Not all teenagers go on to college. The habit of generous giving and volunteering is important in the lives of those who go to work or enter the armed forces after high school; these young people will become the backbone of the work force of America. Habits of generosity and volunteerism, instilled in young adulthood, will help next-generation families and communities grow and prosper, opening wide avenues of interest in their lives. Sharing volunteer time with others helps break down class barriers and overcome prejudices, thus becoming a powerful force for uniting communities. It can also open up opportunities for personal and professional advancement that might have gone unnoticed and help bridge the growing gap between rich and poor.

Teenagers who go on to college will have countless opportunities for service and advocacy. Many colleges now offer degrees in the management of nonprofit institutions, thus validating the importance of philanthropy in modern society. There has been a signficant increase in the number of graduates in social work. Graduate schools at Yale, Indiana, and other institutions of higher education now have programs to study the nonprofit world in depth, encourage research, and publish scholarly reports about philanthropy.

Not long ago, some 120 college presidents formed Campus Compact, which actively promotes public service in undergraduate education. College students are encouraged to volunteer for programs to tutor illiterate adults, build shelters for the homeless, mentor disadvantaged children, and engage in many other types of public service. According to one state governor, at least a million college students are needed for one program alone — tutoring children who are failing in school.

Campus Compact aims to make the service ethic an integral part of undergraduate life. It works with federal, state, and local governments to establish community-service programs; it unites existing efforts, such as teaching adults to read and helping underprivileged children; and it promotes civic involvement on campus. There are thousands of colleges in the United States and Canada, and the energy of young students is boundless. Campus Compact is one way to channel those energies, as are student forums, rallies, political activism and commitment, environmental causes, and work for social justice. The work of students for a better world is an essential part of the social contract of our free society.

According to *USA Today*, college students are going against the spring-break tradition of "beaches, bikinis, and beer," and many volunteer their time to help those less fortunate than they. More than 450 campus chapters of Habitat for Humanity International send thousands of students at spring break to build houses for the poor around the world. Students from the University of Pennsylvania went to Tijuana, Mexico, to build houses in an impoverished area devastated by rain, while forty-three students from Saint

Michael's College in Vermont spent their spring break working with battered women in Washington, D.C. Students from Vanderbilt University went to Guatemala as tutors, while students from Boston College worked with the poor in Boston and Appalachia. What an inspiration to us all!

The Baby Boomers Reach Middle Age

Wealth is a means to an end, not the end itself.
As a synonym for health and happiness, it has had a fair
trial and failed dismally.

JOHN GALSWORTHY

At the end of World War II, the birth rate increased dramatically and remained high for fifteen years. This generation, the "baby boomers," today ranges in age from thirty-seven to fifty-one. Now seventy-five million strong, they account for almost one-third of the adult population of the nation.

The baby boomers are better educated and more prosperous than any previous generation so how they handle their money has far-reaching consequences. According to a recent Independent Sector study, the baby boomers give generously to charity. Those aged thirty-five to forty-four were more likely to make a contribution than any other age group. And the picture is getting brighter — seventy-nine percent of baby boomers made charitable gifts in 1996, up from seventy-six percent in 1987. Their average annual contribution was $956, less than that of people fifty-five to sixty-four ($1,791) but more than young adults twenty-five to thirty-four ($743). The number of volunteer hours put in by baby boomers is also above the national average.

Perhaps the most significant fact about baby boomers is that their parents will, as they die, leave them astonishing amounts of money. Cornell University economist Robert Avery estimates that the baby boomers' parents have accumulated a collective net worth of more than $6.8 trillion. The largest intergenerational transfer of wealth in U.S. history is now underway. If the U.S. economy remains vibrant, the richest one percent of baby boomers will each inherit an average of $1.3 million, the next nine percent an average of $400,000, and the rest an average of $50,000. The richest will become ever richer, but a significant proportion of this money will go to a larger group of about 6 million people.

How will this money be used? Some economists predict that a large amount of this transferred wealth will go directly and quickly to philanthropy. Such a large transfer of wealth to nonprofit organizations might prompt the government to raise inheritance taxes. The federal estate tax now ranges from thirty-seven percent to fifty-five percent. The tendency of state governments, on the other hand, has been to reduce or eliminate inheritance taxes.

How will you benefit if you are a baby boomer who will inherit? Most obviously, you will be more financially secure as you approach your senior years. You will also have a greater opportunity to review your personal, social, political, and spiritual values and to contribute significantly to the causes you believe in. Your gift of time and money can have a tremendous impact on the nation and the world at large. You should begin now to plan what you want to do with your resources so that when the time comes you will be able to act and give effectively.

If you believe that your fortunes will increase significantly through inheritance, you should review your priorities and interests. That way, your wealth can be properly managed. You might wish to ask yourself these questions:

- Have you considered that giving and community service can significantly improve your life?

- What are your most important values, and how might you have a significant and lasting effect on what is important to you?

- How can you take a more active and consistent role in the organizations you believe in?

Some baby boomers have already received their inheritance, and it's interesting to see how they have handled it. An article in the May 1990 issue of Fortune magazine reported on several such heirs: When George Pillsbury inherited $1 million at age forty, he used his fortune to co-found Haymarket People's Fund, a Boston charity that supports groups other charities avoid, such as the El Salvador Sister City Project. Another baby boomer commented, "My grandmother gave to her hospital and zoo, but my generation was politicized through Vietnam, the women's movement, and the gay rights struggle."

Baby boomers have the opportunity to support and endow causes that their new political and social consciousness finds appealing. New types of philanthropies are likely to be beneficiaries of major gifts. What are your values? You may have the opportunity to improve society in a major way by your gift. Causes like the environment, social justice and equality, human rights, peace, and help for the homeless may find new strength and effective impact through your gifts and talents.

Some mainstream charities may suffer from this shift in the patterns of giving, but human needs remain remarkably constant, and as each generation matures, its interests tend to become more conservative and protective. Many radicals of the counterculture have now mellowed. Jerry Rubin, once a national symbol of civil disobedience in the 1960s, became a stockbroker before he died. United Way forecasters believe baby boomers will favor different causes than did their parents and thus change the pattern of distribution of funds to charity and volunteer efforts; however, enduring values and the institutions that represent them will continue to attract strong support.

The Older the Better

What lies behind us and what lies before us are tiny matters compared to what lies within us.

Ralph Waldo Emerson

Older people, especially those between the ages of fifty-five and seventy-five, are more generous than any other age group. They are the backbone of charitable giving. There are some fifty-eight million people in America fifty-five years old or older, more than 57,000 of them over a hundred years old.

Many people's choices as to where they give remain remarkably consistent. A recent article in the *New York Times* described two longtime donors to the *New York Times* Neediest Cases Fund, which began asking for support in 1912. Edith Lissauer, who [died] recently at 100 years of age, had given to the Fund every year since its inception. Hannah Hofheimer, 101, a New Yorker all her life, cannot remember when she didn't support the Neediest Cases Fund. This past year she gave $1,000.

The typical American aged fifty-five to seventy-five donates approximately $1,300 each year to charity. This figure represents about 3.2 percent of annual income, almost 50 percent greater than the national average, which is 2.2 percent. People older than seventy-five tend to give less, perhaps because their assets are smaller or their medical expenses greater, but they still give a fifty percent greater proportion of their income than do people twenty-five to thirty-four years old. According to the Roper Organization, those sixty years or older donated almost $6 billion to nonreligious charities while those eighteen to twenty-nine gave only $2.8 billion.

Older people are also the standard bearers of volunteer activity. Despite their advanced years and sometimes limited health, they are much more likely to volunteer than are younger people. Because they have more time to give, older people give more of their time as volunteers, if sometimes at a more leisurely pace. The elderly are also more positive and traditional in their attitudes about helping others. They recognize that religion and community have sustained them for decades and they feel it is important to repay what they have received.

Let me give you an example. They call themselves the Henhouse Ministry: two dozen women — average age seventy — who have been caring for needy neighbors for more than twenty years. Every Wednesday, the women meet in a single-story farmhouse in Swansea, South Carolina, to quilt, make crafts, and can okra and tomatoes for sale — with their profits they quietly help those in need.

Some people's values shift as they grow older. Friendships, family, community, good health, peace of mind, and spiritual concerns become more important while making money, acquiring showpiece possessions, and succeeding in business enterprise diminish in appeal. This shift from outer-directedness to inner-directedness is a movement away from personal achievement and toward creativity. Philanthropic activity helps older people stay healthy and active.

If stress and tension are the great enemies of the young and ambitious, then isolation, loneliness, and depression are the lurking foes in later life. Many medical and behavioral experts regard volunteer activity as a primary means to guard against physical and mental deterioration. "Stay active," they counsel, "use it or lose it."

We have all seen and marveled at the energetic octogenarian, the spry ninety-year-old who shows up regularly for a volunteer assignment. There are many, like the late Dr. Norman Vincent Peale, who did not feel that reaching ninety-five was any reason to stop serving the community. Mrs. Peale is still active and dynamic, counseling and publishing inspirational books and newsletters. The "graying of America" — the rapid increase in the number of older people — can only have a beneficial effect on giving and volunteering.

T·E·N

PERSONAL POWER: ACTING ALONE
AND TOGETHER

A Path To Greater Personal Power

There can be no greater argument to a man of his own
power than to find himself able not only to accomplish his
own desires, but also to assist other men in theirs; and this is
that conception wherein consisteth charity.

THOMAS HOBBES

How can we create change and make a difference for other people? Since we were children we have all heard about great saints and benefactors of humanity. Newspapers and television inform us about remarkable people who have done wonderful things for others, and we know that goodness, charity, and concern for our neighbors make life better for everyone.

There are, of course, remarkable people of exceptional intelligence, talent, or wealth who do great things. However, the vast majority of present-day miracle workers are ordinary people of limited means. Some of these people are famous throughout the nation and world, while others work quietly and consistently close to home to help their troubled neighbors. All of them change the world.

When I was a child someone told me that most people use only ten percent of their intelligence; as I grew, I wondered how I could use more of the other ninety percent. As time passed, I decided I really didn't have any unusual ability to call upon powers special enough to make a difference in the world, and I more or less dismissed the idea. I think most of us have similar experiences. We have heard of others who have achieved great things, but we see little indication of such powers in our own lives.

Yet many people accomplish so much. They develop successful careers or businesses, achieve financial security, build good marriages, and do a sound job of raising and educating their children, but when they think of helping others they doubt whether they can make much of a difference. This isn't hard to understand. For every book on the powers of giving and sharing, there are fifty on how to succeed in careers. For every college course on community responsibility, there are hundreds on technology and business. We simply haven't spent much energy teaching people how to get in touch with their personal powers to make a difference in the lives of others.

The source of our personal power is our beliefs. What we believe to be true and how we feel about ourselves determine what we think we can do. Our belief system is, to a large extent, a collection of convictions we have about ourselves. If we think we are too weak, too small, too powerless to accomplish anything significant, we limit what we can experience in our lives. If you don't think you can do something, you probably can't.

You have doubtless had the experience of being told that something you wanted to do simply couldn't be done and then seeing someone else do it anyway. So many of our beliefs started out in fear and have held us back ever since. Our fears limit the way we respond to challenges. For every person who, facing a difficulty, says, "Let's work for a miracle," there are ten who will say, "This is impossible." Our attitudes and our beliefs about what we think we can do control what we accomplish. Some of us have walked away from great things in our lives because we were told we weren't capable enough and we believed it. There's a deadening mental exchange, a one-two punch, that can knock out our initiative and genius. Our belief system says, "This is impossible," then our thought process says, "There's no need to get involved; I think I'll go home."

Such preemptive dialogue gives no consideration to the possibility of a miracle. We simply can't exercise our true abilities until we suspend denial of our ability long enough to rise to the occasion. We can become so weighed down by our negative beliefs about ourselves that our personal powers get smothered.

There are people who escape this negativity trap. An ordinary citizen can support a cause out of personal tragedy and force Congress to change the law. A neighbor feels deeply about the plight of the stranded and founds the Travelers Aid Society. A mother loses a child and founds MADD. These people are often astonished at what they have created. At first they may have doubted they could have more than limited local impact, but they were willing to get involved, to make noise, to investigate, to consider the possibilities. Once they moved beyond their own fears, vistas opened up ahead of them. Circumstances changed because they were asking questions, talking to others, looking for advice and support, and planning to change the status quo.

James Chatman doesn't consider himself in the league of Carnegie or Rockefeller, but he does believe he can make a difference. From a bellman at hotels in the segregated South to success as a founder of a business-consulting firm, James was able to acquire some wealth. After retirement, he and his wife decided to make a small difference by establishing a $400,000 Fund at the Northern

Virginia Community Foundation to create a Grandfathers Group to mentor black boys. In his words, "My wife and I really hate the idea of black people seeing ourselves as takers and receivers, and not seeing ourselves as givers."

People like the Chatmans tell me that there comes a point when they begin to believe they can create something new. A dream starts to grow, a conviction that they do have powers to draw on; there's a shift from "what if" to "maybe, if God helps." A kind of spiritual intervention seems to occur that gives them a new faith in their abilities. Dr. Robert Schuller calls it "possibility thinking." These people see themselves in partnership with a spiritual being, then persevere because they believe they and their work are blessed and empowered.

For others the road is less mystical. By making a beginning and letting the situation unfold, their faith in their abilities is confirmed, and they are more and more willing to take risks. M. Scott Peck says of this stage: "Benevolence is community. There can be no community without involvement and no involvement without vulnerability and no vulnerability without risk."

In order to expand our personal powers, we need to suspend what we believe about our limits. We need to set aside negative thoughts about a situation and our ability to change it. We can't help having these limiting thoughts, but that doesn't mean we have to act on them. We need to become involved and investigate, regardless of discouraging, cautionary words — in our own minds or from others. We need to increase our belief in our own potential. We need to have faith in spiritual guidance and support. Finally, we need to be willing to persevere, to be vulnerable, to risk failure.

More than one person who was discouraged about the seeming failure of a business career has told me that when he began to move away from self-interest and toward concern for others, his life, career, and business changed dramatically. His narrow focus on himself had locked up personal power that could only be unleashed when his horizons widened.

Many people yearn to commit themselves to a cause, to give themselves wholly to something worthwhile, few people accomplish this completely. However, in addition to saints, there are millions of ordinary people who have made important contributions simply through dedicated service. You don't need great expertise or sacrifice to produce results. You do need devotion, commitment, willingness, and faith.

When you begin to use your personal power to help others, people benefit from your work. You feel a sense of accomplishment, and your belief in your ability grows. You enjoy things more and have a greater sense of control over your life, which leads to greater self-acceptance and a stronger sense of self-worth. Your physical, emotional, and mental well-being improve. Your vital power becomes an example to others.

The faithful exertion of effort produces all these benefits. While we can certainly use our power for selfish goals, the full range of benefits comes to us only in the accomplishment of good for others. Acts of selfishness may be appealing in the short run but they carry within them the seeds of dissatisfaction and despair.

When you begin to use your personal powers for giving and sharing, you should consider these ways to make your experiences more successful:

- Examine why you have chosen this particular cause and whether it fits your talents.

- Be innovative. Think differently about what you can contribute.

- Be bold, take risks, and think big.

- Talk about your project with everyone. Tell them what you need. You never know where resources — even miracles — will come from.

- Ask for help from friends, relatives, every friendly (and even not-so-friendly) source.

- Put principles and goals before personalities. The world is far from perfect, and people will often disappoint you. Accept others for what they are and move ahead. Be willing to lead.

- Don't drown yourself in your task. Keep your balance. You have a dream: give it your best effort, but also take time to laugh and enjoy life along the way. Smell the flowers. You can reduce stress and attract others with your joy. Turning your goal into a combat mission does not produce harmony and well-being.

- Start out in low gear. Take your time; move with caution and concern for others. Breakneck speed and immediate results are not required. Pace yourself and avoid disillusionment and burnout.

- When you meet an insurmountable obstacle, just sit with it for a while. Get advice from experts. Give your frustration and impatience time to diminish. This may not be easy, but it will save you time, energy, and emotional stress in the long run. Faith and prayer are good partners at such times.

Your attitudes influence the outcome of your efforts at giving. Try to avoid dreams of personal glory. While all act from mixed motives, we can all work to keep them as pure as possible. There's nothing wrong with wanting recognition and praise, but things often go awry when the desires for personal fame, control, or privilege become the primary motives for giving.

Often people enter into charitable work without joy or positive feelings. Some people were brought up to believe that sacrifice, drudgery, duty, and obligation are the components of effective sharing, we believe that if it doesn't hurt, we're not doing it right. These people don't experience the joy and satisfaction inherent in their work or, at best, are indifferent to it.

Acts of generosity should nourish the people who do them. If you aren't getting much satisfaction from your giving efforts, maybe you should look for a cause that would be closer to your heart. There's already enough drudgery and sacrifice in the world, but not nearly enough joy.

If you're a person who just can't seem to get much good feeling out of any activity, maybe you should challenge your ideas about what you're allowed to be in your life. With some courage and willingness, you can have the power to transform your life. The joys in the life of giving and sharing are very real, and you deserve your share of them. As Drs. Robert Ornstein and David Sobel point out in their book *Healthy Pleasures*, altruism is healthy: "The great surprise of human evolution may be that the highest form of selfishness is selflessness."

And what about other people? When you begin to work in a volunteer organization, you're likely to find that people fit into three categories: those who cooperate and support you; those who are indifferent, remote, or unavailable; and those who seem to work at cross-purposes. Also, volunteers are all too human. After a very short time you will come up against the reality that people are on occasion rude, crude, and indifferent, and who are you not to have your feelings hurt? Sometimes frustration and conflict, lack of sensitivity, indifference, and ingratitude will combine to put you on a brittle edge. Working with others requires tolerance and patience particularly when everyone is volunteering their time.

But try a smile, a quiet assurance, a word of praise, and watch how they can defuse conflict. Try not to take yourself or your assignment too seriously. If you do these things and keep a sense of perspective, I promise you that your own personal effectiveness will increase and your cause will prosper.

Some People Who Used Their Personal Powers

The thing which counts is the striving of the human soul to achieve spiritually the best that it is capable of and to care unselfishly not only for personal good, but for the good of all those who toil with them upon the earth.

Eleanor Roosevelt

A Tragedy that Produced A New Law

In April of 1988 Howard and Connie Clery waved good-bye to their lovely nineteen-year-old freshman daughter as she returned to college. Not long after, they received a call telling them she had been brutally raped and murdered in her dormitory room. The couple was devastated and enraged when they found that the ineffectual and closed-mouth campus security force had known the killer to be a campus troublemaker. Out of their grief came a plan: with no formal knowledge of what might be involved, the Clerys put their wrath into action. They lobbied Congress for a federal law making it mandatory that colleges report the numbers and types of crimes committed on campus.

After concerted effort on the part of the Clerys, Congress passed and President Bush signed the Student Right to Know and Campus Security Act of 1990. If colleges fail to provide accurate crime statistics, they risk the loss of federal funds. Now prospective students and their parents can discover the true state of campus security. As Mr. Clery commented, "Hopefully this will help to reduce the scourge of violence on our college campuses, much of which is committed by students because of drug and alcohol abuse."

Here is a couple who was moved to action by their personal tragedy. They used their energies to get Congress to pass a law that will lessen the likelihood of other parents experiencing a loss like theirs. They saw the national implications in their personal loss and had the courage, determination, and willingness to take the steps necessary to change the status quo. Many lives may be saved as a result.

Answered Prayers and Then Some

According to a *New York Times* story, Cheryl Woods, a Kansas City nurse, lost her paycheck just before Christmas. The $400 check was already endorsed and could have been cashed by whoever found it. It was found by Rosemary Pritchett, a homeless mother of three young children, who had just put in a bid on an abandoned house with the little money she had left. Mrs. Pritchett said it never crossed her mind to cash the check. She looked up Mrs. Woods's phone number from the address printed on the check and used her last quarter to make the call.

When Mrs. Woods came to pick up the check, she found the Pritchetts in a homeless shelter and she offered a $25 reward. Mrs. Pritchett declined, saying, "Just give me a note of thanks I can show my children. I want them to know that when you find something, somebody has lost it." Only when Mrs. Woods threatened to leave the $25 on the floor and walk away did Mrs. Pritchett accept the reward.

The next day Mrs. Pritchett's bid on the abandoned house was accepted and she moved her children and few possessions into a house that was little more than a shell. The walls were crumbling, and vandals had ripped out the wires and plumbing. A few days later, Mrs. Woods visited and found the Pritchetts trying to repair the house with only a hammer and screwdriver. She decided to do something about the situation.

The first thing she did was to ignore her husband's warning that the job would break her heart. She took up the Yellow Pages, worked her way through the contractor section, and finally found a contractor who agreed to become supervisor without charge. Another contractor offered to install a free water heater, and a supplier built windows and donated fixtures. Mrs. Woods's retired uncle also worked on the restoration.

When newspapers and television picked up the story, the project began to take on a life of its own. Contractors and builders offered free labor and equipment. Debris was removed free and total strangers came forward to help. In the end, $30,000 worth of labor and equipment were donated. It all happened because one person cared enough to help a neighbor who had helped her, and everyone benefited.

Linda and Millard Fuller founded Habitat for Humanity International on this same principles, neighbor helping neighbor. Believing that everyone on this planet should have a decent place in which to live, they founded Habitat for Humanity in 1976: By the year 2000, more than 100,000 homes will have been built for the poor around the world by thousands of volunteers who believe that helping others help themselves is really what it is all about.

The Magic of Youth

Brian O'Connell, in his book *Volunteers in Action*, tells how young Trevor Ferrell was watching television on a cold December night in 1983; the news showed Philadelphia street people huddled over steam vents to stay warm. Trevor pleaded with his father to take him downtown so that he could deliver a blanket and pillow. This single visit became a nightly mission of mercy. As word of Trevor's generosity spread, contributions from all over the country poured in to what became known as Trevor's Campaign. Some 250 volunteers now cook and deliver soup and sandwiches nightly to the homeless. A thirty-three-bedroom rooming house, anonymously donated, is being renovated as a day shelter for one hundred homeless people. Trevor, now twenty years old, focused attention on the needs of homeless people and showed the nation the difference one young person can make.

At Home At Last

For many years Robert Hayes, thirty-two, has visited homeless shelters and appeared in court to prod New York City into providing places for homeless people to sleep. This advocate for the homeless sued the city in 1979 and obtained a consent decree to provide clean, safe shelter to every homeless person who seeks it. In 1982 he founded the Coalition for the Homeless, which has grown into three national organizations. The Coalition's activities include running a camp for homeless children and feeding thousands of people every day.

Giving and Caring Keep Us Going

In 1988 Arnolta Williams received the President's Volunteer Action Award. At ninety-one, she had devoted seventy years to helping the poor and uneducated youth of Jacksonville, Florida. She was a founder of the Jacksonville Urban League and the founder of the Gateway Nursery, which serves low-income working mothers. She had volunteered for the Red Cross, the Council on Aging, the ywca, and had been chairperson on the Foster Grandparents Program, a board member of Florida Community College, a member of the Mayor's Commission on the Status of Women, and a delegate to the 1981 White House Council on Aging. She had spent her life helping the young, the old, the poor, and the uneducated. Her energy and personal powers made her a remarkable woman.

Dreams That Fly

Dale Shields, a Floridian who moved from Michigan in 1975, has saved more than 16,000 pelicans and other birds hurt or disabled by boats, fishhooks, pesticides, automobiles, and other man-made hazards. At first his efforts were random and limited; he loved the beauty of the pelican and he wanted to do more, but he didn't have the time and resources. When he realized he couldn't help all the birds by himself, he began to ask around and decided to risk starting a nonprofit organization — the Pelican Man's Bird Sanctuary, a bird and wildlife refuge. From a part-time one-man effort, his dream has become a 4,000-member organization with 150 volunteers who rescue and care for birds at the sanctuary. In 1990 President Bush cited him as one of the "Points of Light." Dale says he appreciated the citation but was even more pleased by a letter from a twelve-year-old who told him that she was so inspired by his work that she plans to become a veterinarian.

Lumpy Willie

When William was five years old, his seemingly normal body began to change. Lumps developed on his forehead and neck and soon spread to his hands and back. Diagnosed as Von Recklinghausen's disease (a form of neurofibromatosis), the odd-shaped fibroid tumors soon completely covered his body. He quickly picked up the nickname "Lumpy Willie." To compound his misery, his parents both died when he was twelve, leaving him alone with his physical nightmare.

As a teenager, he met with cruel rejection. No girl would go out with him. Restaurant waitresses hated to serve him. He refused to look at himself in a mirror. Life got worse and worse for Lumpy Willie, "The Ugliest Man in Canada."

To numb his misery, he turned first to alcohol and then to other drugs. His anger and desperation led him into crime: By the time he was twenty-one he had been arrested more than fifty times for petty theft and finally for armed robbery. At twenty-five, he was sent to prison for life. Rejected by his fellow inmates, he spent much of his prison time in solitary confinement.

Darrell Davis, a resident in neurosurgery, heard of Willie's predicament. Eager to experiment with a new surgical procedure that held out some hope for victims like Willie, Dr. Davis asked for an interview with him. He was flatly denied; Willie's bitterness had closed all doors of hope for him. However over a period of month, Dr. Davis's persistence paid off. Willie met with him and, after several conversations, consented to a limited surgical experiment on his face. Over the next twelve months, Dr. Davis performed sixteen operations in more than thirty hours of surgery. He worked obsessively, at no charge, to liberate Willie from his personal prison.

On Willie's birthday in July of 1963, Dr. Davis came to his cell with a brightly wrapped gift. When the paper was torn away Willie found himself looking in a mirror and was unable to believe what he saw: a normal man with a normal face. He cried. He laughed. He hugged his benefactor. Willie wasn't lumpy any more!

The change in his life was immediate, and he became a model prisoner. Within six months, he and Dr. Davis stood before a judge and heard him declare Willie a free man, returning him to society to begin a new life. From then until his death four-and-a-half years later from internal complications from the disease, the man once known as "The Ugliest Man in Canada" was one of its outstanding citizens. Dr. Davis's gift of skill, work, and hope not only brought new life to a condemned man; it also initiated an unending wellspring of joy in the young doctor's life.

Daily Use of Personal Powers

As part of the White House's Points of Light Initiative to encourage volunteerism, President Bush in the early 1990s honored individuals, nonprofit groups, and companies that were "making a difference in their communities. Some of the people and groups cited by the Points of Light Initiative included:

- Justin Lebo, Saddle Brook, New Jersey, a thirteen-year-old who rebuilds old bicycles for needy children. He runs a lemonade stand, saves his allowance, and collects donations to raise money to purchase bike parts.

- Florence Ziedman, Buffalo Grove, Illinois, who began volunteering for the Hines Veterans Administration hospital in Hines, Illinois, during World War II and still visits patients at the hospital today.

- Volunteers of Lakeview Shepherd Center, New Orleans, Louisiana, who offer assistance to senior citizens, such as rides to doctors appointments and food delivery.

- Minerva Soerheide, Mount Hermon, California, who devotes at least forty hours each week to tutoring adults in English, including workplace literacy, reading, and writing. Ms. Soerheide also tutors Hispanics trying to obtain U.S. citizenship.

- Mitchell Cardell Baldwin, Birmingham, Alabama, who, after growing up in a housing project, founded CHAMP (Caring Helps Another Make Progress), which provides positive role models and weekly activities for young people in a neighborhood housing project.

- Connie Harris, Springfield, Oregon, who, drawing on her own experience as a teenage parent, volunteers as leader of the Birth to Three support group, which encourages young mothers to continue their education and helps them become better parents.

- Davarian Baldwin, Beloit, Wisconsin, a teenager who for three years has been a member of the Beloit Positive Youth Development program, which helps young people in low-income neighborhoods appreciate their community and the environment. He founded a rap group that offers advice to young people, is the president of the Urban 4-H program, and each summer leads a camping trip for city youths.

- Gudrun Gaskill, Golden, Colorado, who in 1972 began to help build the Colorado Trail, a string of hiking paths and campsites which spans 470 miles. Today, Ms. Gaskill, sixty-three, coordinates the volunteer work crews, handles all paperwork, and still helps with the physical labor of improving the trail.

- Harvest House, Lansing, Michigan, whose volunteers search the streets for the homeless and inform them about Harvest House programs such as hot-meal services and substance-abuse education.

- Ron Dickey, El Paso, Texas, a quadriplegic who volunteers twenty hours a week for DARE (Disabled Ability Resource Environment), offering disabled people advice and friendship.

- David Goldstein, Albany, New York, who volunteers nights for the Samaritans, a suicide-prevention program, and helps recruit additional volunteers.

- John L. Oliver, Midland, Texas, a retired engineer who drives seventy miles every Friday to the West Texas Children's Home to tutor children in mathematics.

- Volunteers of Rosemont Center, Columbus, Ohio, who provide counseling and job-skills training, as well as assistance with support groups and field trips, to the adolescent girls at this residential and daycare facility.

- Volunteers of Community Service Project, Rockland, Maine, where one hundred young people help the elderly and disabled with home repairs and maintenance.

- Clare Allen, Nashville, Tennessee, a volunteer for the Harris Hillman School who tutors disabled children daily and helps them with physical therapy and other living skills.

- William Smith, Donora, Pennsylvania, a seventy-seven-year-old who helps his neighbor, a divorced mother of two children living on a fixed income, by providing transportation and buying the family food, clothing, and school supplies.

Some 1,020 people received the Points of Light honor when George Bush was president. The program has been recently reactivated by President Bill Clinton and the award is given daily to such people as:

- Tess Wise, Maitland, Florida, founder and executive director of the Holocaust Memorial Resource and Education Center of Central Florida and creator of prejudice-reduction educational programs and curricula that are used through-out the country.

- Audrey E. Evans, Philadelphia, a physician who in 1974 founded the first Ronald McDonald House, of which there are now 175 worldwide.

- Ron Gonzales, San Jose, California, who created the Role Model Program, which encourages middle-school students to look to business and community leaders as inspirational mentors.

These are just a few of the many people who use their personal powers to make the world better for others. They are the people we are talking about in this book — people who have sought and found a meaningful life through sharing. Don't you want to be one of them?

Self-Help and Support Groups

Through the community of AA and similar fellowships
modeled on it, millions upon millions have received healing,
millions upon millions have found meaning in their lives.
No other phenomenon has had such an
impact for good in a nation.

M. SCOTT PECK

We are a troubled society, beset by internal and external pressures. One of the best remedies we have discovered for our troubles is the support group. Millions of people have found peer support groups to be an amazingly successful path to recovery, whether from alcoholism, cancer, or divorce. The National Self-Help Clearinghouse in New York City estimates that there are at least 500,000 self-help groups serving fifteen million members.

The proliferation of support groups is a uniquely American reaction to personal crisis. People in trouble can turn to others with similar difficulties. The support-group phenomenon is pure philanthropy: suffering people welcoming others and offering love, compassion, and assistance. Every available statistic shows that support groups help people make real and lasting change. Most groups are made up of people in similar circumstances coming together to share experience, information, and emotional support; those who simply listen often get as much out of the experience as those who actively participate.

Several features are basic to all self-help groups. First, participation is limited to people who have experienced the kind of suffering the group exists to alleviate. There are no salaried leaders who make wise pronouncements based on professional knowledge. There are no lectures, only people sharing their personal experience with other people. There is no hierarchy, only a very rudimentary organization in which everyone enjoys equal status.

Second, the responsibility for change and recovery rests squarely on the individual member. The groups provide a supportive environment where change and growth can take place, but each member is the architect of his or her own recovery. The self-help movement stresses tangible results. It rests on a very American assumption: bring together the resources, take responsibility for the problem, and solve it.

The self-help movement began in 1935 with the founding of Alcoholics Anonymous. In 1950 AA was followed by ALANON, a self-help group for spouses and children and parents of alcoholics. In recent years, awareness of the many problems that can best be solved through concerned support has caused the number of self-help groups to skyrocket. There are now groups focusing on divorce, drug dependency problems, isolation and loneliness among single and elderly people, mental illness, life-threatening diseases, and compulsions ranging from gambling and overeating to shoplifting, sex, and workaholism. Victims of diseases, rape, incest, and drunk driving have come together, as have abusive parents, parents of runaway children, and recently released felons. People of various minority groups band together for mutual support. Although by definition the membership in an anonymous group cannot be accurately tallied, estimates place the membership in AA at two million, with Adult Children of Alcoholics (ACOA) and ALANON not far behind.

There are four basic categories of support groups:

- Addictions such as alcohol, drugs, food, gambling, and work.

- Illnesses both physical and mental, from cancer and heart disease to schizophrenia and phobias.
- Personal crises, from divorce, widowhood, and the death of a child to physical abuse and incest.
- Relatives and friends of people with serious problems, (such as ALANON, ACOA, AL-TEEN), and the parents of suicidal children.

There is a positive relationship between self-help groups and more general kinds of volunteering and charitable giving. A ten-year study at Stanford University showed that terminally ill cancer patients who participated in weekly support groups survived for a period nearly twice as long as those who did not. Consistent participation in self-help groups will teach a member to care for other people; as with philanthropic activity, people heal themselves while helping to heal others. For millions of people self-help groups dispel loneliness and isolation and help focus concern on other people.

A more conservative fiscal policy has recently led to large cutbacks in government spending for social services. Support groups cannot meet all these needs, but they help focus the intelligence and compassion of individual people on real problems and frequently lead to solutions. Given the realities of our economy, they may be the backbone of social progress for years to come. People who successfully manage their problems and who are aware of similar problems in others are much more likely to volunteer, give to a cause, and work for its success. Another study indicates that as many as forty percent of all people in the "helping professions" came from troubled families and have triumphed over their own problems, often with the help of self-help and support groups.

How do you join this effort? Examine your life. Perhaps you are already aware of a problematic area. Look around; ask about groups dealing with your situation. If you can't find one, start one. All you need is a room to meet in, a little publicity, an hour or so to spare on a regular basis, and enough love and concern to share yourself with others in similar need. You can change the world while you change your own life.

E·L·E·V·E·N

EMERGENCE OF
GLOBAL PROBLEMS

The Global Need for Giving

*Help thy brother's boat across, and lo thine own
has reached the shore.*

HINDU PROVERB

Older generations tend to view philanthropy as traditional charity, in other words, giving to the disadvantaged to eliminate suffering; younger people are more apt to see it as a complex system, with government bearing chief responsibility and private initiative providing special assistance. Clearly, neither the state nor private initiative can eliminate or even alleviate poverty, suffering, and social injustice single-handedly. The job requires a progressive, sensitive society in which personal commitment helps provide the resources for many basic needs. Philanthropy, working through its many different channels, can demonstrate ways to resolve social ills.

Perhaps a quarter of the planet's population has a woefully inadequate standard of living. Adequate food and shelter, clothing, medical care, and literacy are beyond the reach of billions. They live in grinding, searing poverty, where simple survival dominates their lives. All countries, even the most advanced, have citizens who suffer poverty, illiteracy, discrimination, and disenfranchisement, but the severity of conditions and the ability of both government and private citizens to respond to these needs vary greatly from country to country.

For the sake of contrast, consider Cleveland, Ohio, and a typical village in Ethiopia. Cleveland, which has an illiteracy rate of seven percent or eight percent also has millions of well-educated residents and thousands of teachers, schoolrooms that are empty at night, community centers, funds for books and paper and, the capability, should enough citizens exert themselves, to end illiteracy almost overnight.

A typical village in the highlands of Ethiopia probably has an illiteracy rate of seventy percent. The country is torn by civil war, drought, famine, oppressive government control, poverty, high infant mortality, and a crumbling ecosystem. There is no government support for books, paper, pencils, or schoolrooms. Some of the population is literate but only at a rudimentary level; certainly few citizens are able to instruct. The government uses much of its money for the military, which leaves very little to train and deploy teachers. The only substantial philanthropic structure is based on governmental foreign aid and assistance from such groups as OXFAM, CARE, UNICEF, Christian Aid, World Vision, and Save the Children, but neither governments nor philanthropic groups such as these can resolve the problem of illiteracy.

Large populations in many countries all over the world suffer chronic poverty. The governments of most of these countries are virtually powerless. They lack the resources and sometimes the commitment to raise their own people's standard of living. Private philanthropy in these countries is limited, personal, and often misunderstood.

Public benevolence in all countries is shaped by local and regional cultural values, economics, and religious customs. In North America the roots of civic virtue are in religion. Citizens demonstrate their benevolence by giving of their money, talent, and time. In some Asian cultures, charity is based on the family and is largely extended to relatives and the community, in the form of loans and guidance for local businesses or family members in need. Very few people think in terms of national or global responsibility.

Yet people in all cultures have an almost natural urge to help others in distress. This tendency can be fostered, as it is in many advanced societies or blunted, in societies where the struggle to satisfy even the most primitive needs occupies all of human existence, but virtually all people experience a conscious or unconscious struggle between self-interest and compassion for others, between acquisition and generosity.

In economically limited societies, people who share usually give time and effort rather than money. The generous cooperation of people in third-world countries often astonishes visitors from developed nations. Sri Lanka, off the south coast of India, is a rural agricultural nation with a per-capita annual income of perhaps $400, yet philanthropy is very much a part of this indigenous culture. People regularly give their time to public projects or to assist their neighbors. A good deal of aid comes from worldwide organizations, but the programs are staffed and run by thousands of local volunteers. The people think in terms of national needs.

Some African nations, on the other hand, are deeply divided by tribal and regional loyalties that restrict their sense of responsibility for others. The primary unit of loyalty is the tribal group; all resources are acquired for the tribe, and the suffering of a neighboring group is none of their concern. While there is a high level of sharing within the group, there is little cooperative spirit between tribes. Not surprisingly, competition, even war, is often the normal state of affairs.

Christianity and Islam as well as supratribal governmental action can broaden these tribal loyalties to include others, but sometimes even these forces are harnessed in support of tribal competition. In the future, as tribal communities move to embrace each other, the possibilities will increase for social change through philanthropy. This reality may now seem a long way off in Africa, but the knowledge that it is possible is incentive enough to bring the joy of giving to the lives of many Africans.

There is no possibility that governments can meet all the enormous needs of poorer nations. Philanthropic action is the mainstay for much, if not most, improvement in the lives of people in many parts of the world. The necessity for giving and sharing on the global level has never been higher than it is now. I can see three classes of nations, divided according to natural resources, industrial capacity, and standard of living. Each has different levels and forms of civic idealism and philanthropic urgency.

Industrially Advanced Nations

Western Europe, North America, Japan, Korea, Israel, Australia and New Zealand, Saudi Arabia, and some Latin American nations are technologically advanced. Most of them have a high standard of living and an effective central government with some form of capitalist economy. They have a strong sense of community responsibility and, in some of them, philanthropy flourishes. They also give to help other developing nations; to some extent, their philanthropic approach is global.

Industrially Developing Nations

Most of Latin America, Eastern Europe, North Africa, China, Turkey, South Africa, North Korea, and some countries in Southeast Asia have emerging economies, substantial resources, and a decent — if modest — standard of living for most of their people. They also have substantial poverty and disenfranchisement, large rural and agrarian populations, partial literacy at best, and rudimentary social services. For most of these nations, philanthropy is internal and less generous, primarily because of their lower standard of living. Most human-service activities are carried out by volunteers on a local level only. Governments vary in strength and effectiveness, and political upheaval often hampers social progress. Many of these countries depend on outside aid; they are limited in what they can export to help others and often have enormous debt to more advanced nations. Russia also has to contend with revolt, insufficient resources, aged equipment, and widespread corruption.

Underdeveloped Nations

Albania, Sudan, Kampuchea, Vietnam, Lebanon, Central Africa, much of India, Pakistan, Afghanistan, and Somalia are some of the most disadvantaged nations. They are chronically beset by war, famine, drought, political upheaval, primitive economies, plundered ecosystems, limited natural resources, widespread illiteracy, unmanageable government debt, runaway population growth, and tragically inadequate health care. These nations have only the most basic and direct public benevolence, with people helping each other to survive.

Charitable organizations from many advanced countries supply basic human needs, yet demand for goods and services far outstrips the supply. Money and resources are scarce, but human compassion is plentiful: The late Mother Teresa's India missions for the poor are one example of the kind of local service possible with help from international giving. In most of these countries, civic service focuses on community and individual family needs. Their countries, disrupted by war, famine, and overpopulation, lack the resources to raise the standard of living substantially. Some, in fact, experience a continuous decline in living standards.

The world press provides stark, realistic accounts of the stresses faced by individuals, families, and communities in the underdeveloped nations. Advanced nations are thus made more and more aware of the complex and chronic nature of these problems. Relief and development organizations provide aid, but the demand for assistance far exceeds the available contributions of money, resources, and technology.

Some underdeveloped nations have promising resources that could, over time, help them become self-sufficient. Other countries are too overpopulated, resource-poor, or economically paralyzed to be able to achieve self-sufficiency on their own. One of the challenges for aid and development organizations is the problem of how best to allocate funds and resources, particularly when available resources can meet only limited immediate needs — survival has to be weighed against self-sufficiency efforts. The problem is further compounded by weak and poor governments that plunder or mismanage foreign aid to ensure continued political control. Emerging economies, supported by huge philanthropic outlays, are sometimes devastated by political self-interest and the corruption of their leaders.

All nations, not just the poorer ones must deal with poverty and illiteracy, abuse of human rights, environmental pollution, and ecosystem destruction. To resolve these problems, both government and concerned citizens need to band together. Where governments falter, private initiative, local charities, and national advocacy must step in and shoulder the burden.

Most contributions by individuals are earmarked for domestic use. It seems that most people follow the rule of "charity begins at home," with "home" being defined as within a forty-mile radius; donations to the United Way and the collections of church organizations are almost always dispersed locally. Data from a recent survey suggests that donations by Americans to international relief may not exceed $200 million, a small sum compared to U.S. foreign aid. Religious donations may exceed this amount, but it is difficult to know the extent to which religious funds find their way overseas as development aid and relief.

In disadvantaged countries and in the poverty-stricken regions of developing nations, calamity and chaos are more enduring than international philanthropy, disease and despair more prevalent than health and hope. As global economic and ecological systems deteriorate, the plight of underdeveloped countries will worsen. Human need will escalate.

The developing nations will also suffer for many years to come from the burden of borrowing to become self-sufficient and to advance technologically. As taxes increase and rural unemployment grows, some of the resources for community human services will shrink. This will interrupt many service programs, slow the movement toward self-sufficiency, and increase the ranks of the poor. Few countries have the oil of Venezuela, Nigeria, or Indonesia, or precious metal reserves like those in South Africa; most nations put their investment into agricultural enterprises. These economies are subject to fluctuating prices on the international market and the vagaries of the weather, debt reduction, political unrest, ravaged ecosystems, and shifts in demand for agricultural products will limit the development of many countries for the foreseeable future.

Charitable giving is an important part of public and private life in most of Europe, North America, and some Asian countries, but the charity of the rich nations cannot cope with the poverty and other needs of developing countries. As problems in these countries increase, advanced nations will doubtless become more ambivalent about a larger global commitment and revert to more insulated charity that benefits their own community. However, all nations need to be concerned about their suffering neighbors. We cannot, in the twenty-first century, walk away from our ever-expanding responsibilities. We need to become globally philanthropic, both as individuals and as nations.

Government, Economics, and Cultural Values

*Each of us will one day be judged by our
standard of life — not by our standard of living;
by our measure of giving — not by our measure of wealth;
by our simple goodness — not by our seeming greatness.*

WILLIAM ARTHUR WARD

Benevolence is heavily influenced by government policy, the state of the economy, and cultural values. Government can assume the role of enlightened enabler and provider or it can seriously discourage private initiative. A downturn in the economy can dry up funds available for giving. A community's cultural values can shape the nature and content of giving and volunteerism. Limited vision and exclusionary practices can deeply restrict both aid to underdeveloped countries and domestic service. Let's look more closely at how some of these factors affect a nation's philanthropic behavior.

Government Influence

Governments are often inconsistent, greedy, and oppressive. At times they reflect the will of the people who gave them power; at other times, they march to their own tune. In almost all nations, the government is the largest contributor to the national welfare. In order to serve, support, and rule, governments levy taxes that can range from fair and equitable to suffocating. Taxes can favor business enterprise but penalize workers, make it easy to accumulate wealth or be so restrictive that the acquisition of any wealth is impossible. Tax policies can favor redistribution of wealth to serve the population or further enhance the fortunes of the mega-rich.

In Japan, tax policy makes it difficult for powerful businessmen to accumulate great personal wealth. In some oil-rich Middle East nations, a handful of leaders may own the majority of the nation's assets and have personal fortunes in the billions. While it's true that much of this accumulated wealth is shared with other people in benevolent gestures and funds for services, there are those who would question the right of anyone to amass great wealth that does not circulate for the good of all. A serious imbalance in wealth often produces a two-class state consisting of the super-rich and the multitudinous poor. A benevolent and responsive government, can do a great deal to foster philanthropy and volunteerism, but the task is more difficult when much of the population is impoverished, the government is financially overextended by borrowing from other nations, or the super-rich — like the late President Marcos of the Philippines — are driven by consummate greed.

There are many ways for government policy to encourage the overall climate for philanthropy. Tax exemption for gifts made to charity is perhaps the most obvious. In the United States, tax exemption for philanthropic gifts is a historic tradition; in Japan, it is a new experiment. A host of other incentives can be employed to reward and support private "nongovernmental organizations," or NGOs. Most governments recognize the value of NGOs to the disadvantaged population. Indeed, the NGOs are the lifeblood of many developing nations, converting donations into services and administering international aid and relief.

Sometimes governments rely on NGOs to do the whole job for them, but there are even more situations in which governments attempt to guide and control the substance and form of public endeavor too closely. Misguided governments occasionally try to use NGOs and their services to fill in gaps left by their inconsistency or corruption. To be most effective, the nonprofit sector must be free to use its resources as it sees fit, independently assessing needs and attempting to meet them in its own unique way.

Governments sometimes become suspicious of foreign aid. Relief supplies funneled into a war-torn region can end up in unintended hands; peasants in a struggling socialist country may be influenced by relief sent by a democratic nation; medical and religious volunteers, missionaries, or technologists may be viewed as a security threat by an edgy regime; any form of educational support, be it domestic or foreign, will be carefully scrutinized by insecure or suspicious governments. International organizations may even be forbidden to bring relief to a starving ethnic or political group because the government's design is to starve the group to death or force them to become refugees. In such settings it is difficult for any form of philanthropy to serve people's needs.

Philanthropy has occasionally been politicized by well-meaning citizens, foreign governments, and international religious movements. In countries where the heavy hand of government control is everywhere, many spontaneous reactions to urgent needs are stifled. Both contributions and volunteer activity are carefully controlled or discouraged. People who live in truly democratic nations are fortunate to be able to share and give with little or no interference from the government. While human-rights issues and environmental conflicts are sometimes problematic even in the freest nations, we in the United States are generally free to pursue whatever causes we believe in.

Influence of Economics

If religion is the mother of philanthropy, economics is a close member of the family. While great feats have been accomplished with little more than modest personal gifts and volunteer labor, most philanthropy involves substantial amounts of money and so is influenced by economic conditions. America has a fundamentally sound economy in which more than ninety percent of our able-bodied citizens are employed. The peaks and troughs of the economic cycle have not had a long-lasting impact since World War II. There have been declines in a number of industries, but most economic change has been accompanied by some form of economic remedy. Because the American economy is relatively stable — though sometimes sluggish — American giving has increased every year for the last thirty years.

In many nations the relatively stable American economy and relatively high standard of living are greatly envied. Economic downturns and financial upheavals that would paralyze Americans if they occurred here regularly afflict many nations. Fickle world demand for various commodities, natural disasters such as flood and drought, and runaway inflation turn millions of people into paupers overnight. Shifts in demand for raw materials leave entire populations destitute and anxious to migrate.

All of these factors influence the willingness of a people to share resources with disadvantaged neighbors. Giving and volunteer activity are almost impossible when entire families have to work six days a week simply to put food on the table. There is little time to help anyone, except perhaps family members. As an economic climate worsens, people have less to give, are less inclined to be generous to those people outside their family or community, have little time to volunteer, and are unlikely to consider the needs of others in their own country, much less foreign nations. Where the economy has collapsed, most financial generosity simply evaporates except on the part of the very wealthy; even the government cannot provide services when there is little revenue. This situation is far more common than you might think.

An energetic philanthropic system can bring about great changes in living standards, education, and health. When a nation has valuable resources, a sound economy, and a growing national output, that nation can raise funds to help eliminate illiteracy and lower infant mortality. Orphanages can be built; technical assistance can be provided to improve agriculture, cottage industries can be encouraged; and human-rights problems can be investigated and remedied.

A healthy business climate spurs all sectors of a nation. NGOs can help bring about self-sufficiency in distressed areas; education liberates millions from drudgery; and governments can afford to provide services to increase the standard of living of the entire population. In a healthy economy, optimism and energy abound.

Cultural Values

One simple but powerful example of how cultural values affect philanthropy can be seen in Western Europe, where religion and philosophy have long emphasized service, charity, and compassion. For hundreds of years, benevolent acts have been encouraged and admired and social responsibility has been taught in classrooms and within the family. When millions of Europeans emigrated to the United States, they brought these traditions with them. The American philanthropic tradition owes an extraordinary debt to Western European religious and cultural values that encourage brotherhood, sharing, and private response to the needs of the disadvantaged.

In Africa, cultural values are quite different and lead to a different flow of philanthropy and good deeds. The local village or tribe commands and nurtures loyalty. Commitment to family and extended family are prevalent; a more universal view of human need and suffering is not. This narrower approach is helpful for the survival and preservation of tribal groups but does little to support a broader effort.

In Asia, the recent economic growth and dominant commercial stature of Japan, Korea, and China have created a shift in cultural values. In much of Asia, the great new wealth is largely controlled by corporations, and a sense of corporate responsibility for the public welfare is growing, particularly in Japan. With the emergence of these highly productive nations as world entrepreneurs, the state of world philanthropy is beginning to shift. These Far East nations are more willing to aid disadvantaged countries and to contribute to domestic organizations working to bring about a better standard of living, education, and human rights for all.

Pressures Are Mounting

So many paths that wind and wind,
While just the art of being kind,
Is all the sad world needs.

ELLA WHEELER WILCOX

Resources and People

The world is in trouble. Economic, social, and ecological systems can no longer keep pace with changes in the global situation. Dozens of world issues increase in scope and severity while our capacity to deal with them seems to diminish. Years ago U Thant, Secretary General of the United Nations, said, "The members of the United Nations have perhaps ten years left in which to subordinate their ancient quarrels and launch a global partnership to curb the arms race, improve the human environment, defuse the population explosion, and supply the required momentum to development efforts. If such a global partnership is not forged . . . then I very much fear that the problems I have mentioned will have reached such staggering proportions that they will be beyond our capacity to control."

More than ten years have passed, and we still seem incapable of rising above our differences. War, civil war, and revolution ravage nations and cripple what tenuous economic and educational progress has been made. International forums that exist to resolve disputes are rarely used. Lebanon, Bosnia, Iran, Iraq, Vietnam, Kampuchea, E1 Salvador, Ethiopia, Sudan, Somalia, and Bangladesh all suffer social, economic, and ecological devastation; their citizens are enslaved, driven out, or reduced to mere survival. Ten or twenty years of progress are callously wiped out by war. Strife, conquest, and plunder seem almost genetic in origin.

The superpowers and other developed nations spend staggering proportions of their tax revenues to support their war machines. Think of the good that could be done if what is spent on the military were redirected to social and environmental problems — but fears both real and illusory and the delusions of might and power keep defeating this potential first aid for a sick planet.

Wealth and resources are not equitably distributed throughout the world. As much as seventy percent of the world's wealth is concentrated in countries with less than fifteen percent of the planet's population. This dramatic imbalance takes a heavy toll.

Some areas of the globe are more richly endowed by nature than others. Oil, gold and other precious metals, fertile soil, temperate climate, friendly weather patterns, and vital minerals bless some regions and not others. Social progress, educational advances, and a favorable population distribution favor some areas over others. These factors have created significant differences in living standards between nations: the rich get richer and the poor are further exploited.

This process is accelerating. Since the beginning of the Industrial Revolution in the late eighteenth century, raw materials and scarce resources have been found and plundered by powerful industrial nations. Countries with large oil deposits and advanced technological capabilities have recently acquired enormous wealth, which only increases the fiscal imbalance as both oil and technology are needed by poorer countries for development. The issue of the imbalance of wealth and resources has generated a great deal of ideological and diplomatic conflict. It would be unrealistic to propose that the five wealthiest nations — Japan, the United States, Germany, Saudi Arabia, and the United Kingdom — invest ten percent of their wealth in the fifty poorest nations, yet it would take an effort of such proportions to bring about meaningful change.

Many efforts have been made to spur development, beginning with the Marshall Plan after World War II, and progress has been made, notably in Japan, Germany, France, Mexico, Korea, and China. However, many nations lack the resources, technical capability, and political stability to break the cycle of ineffective economy, revolution, war, poverty, environmental plunder, and runaway population growth.

In 1900 there were 1.6 billion people on the planet. Present estimates place world population at about 4.5 billion — in less than a century the population has nearly tripled. In the next thirty to forty years the population will reach eight billion people, many (if not most) of whom will be living in poverty. Even with government-sponsored birth-control programs in populous countries such as India and China, the global birthrate has not effectively slowed.

Perhaps as many as twenty-five million people die from starvation and water-borne disease every year, many of them young children; UNICEF says that some 45,000 infants die from starvation every day. Clearly we are not able to provide for the vast increases in world population. Religious and cultural beliefs that oppose birth control make the problem even more difficult; some say governments have no right to limit the freedom to reproduce. Illiteracy and poor medical care also hinder efforts at population control. Tragically, the key restraints on population growth in the world today are famine, disease, and war.

Many other social ills plague our planet, from war and economic devastation to racial and cultural discrimination, widespread violation of human rights, inadequate medical care, illiteracy and unequal access to education, inadequate housing, and corrupt and ineffective governments. And soaring birthrates are commonplace in all but the most advanced nations.

The Environment

The twentieth century has callously polluted the three basic elements that sustain life: air, water, and soil. Industrial use of raw materials, fueled by the population explosion, has laid waste to vast areas of the planet. We are in effect attacking our own biosphere, the interconnected habitat of all life on earth. Near the end of a century of indifference, we are awakening to the realization that modern civilization has created a broad range of ecological crises. We must change our behavior if we are to halt or reverse these changes. It will take time, restraint, and enormous amounts of money. Virtually every nation is guilty to some degree of ecological degradation, but the most highly industrialized nations have been the most destructive.

The ozone layer in the upper atmosphere which protects the earth and its inhabitants from the sun's ultraviolet light is being steadily eroded by industrial chemicals. Oxygen-producing forests are cut down at alarming rates, and increased carbon dioxide in the upper atmosphere has already begun the deservedly feared process of global warming. Some scientists estimate that a one percent increase in global warming will raise the height of oceans enough to inundate many coastal cities.

Energy production continues to pour pollutants into the air we breathe, increasing the toxins in our lungs and blood. Airborne pollution creates acid rain, which is already killing lakes and rivers and threatening entire water systems, if not the oceans themselves. Nutrient supplies in the water are being undermined by oil and other mineral pollutants. Ocean fish, a primary food source for millions, contain ever-higher levels of mercury and other toxins. In 1974 the Ford Foundation Energy Project concluded that a point of no return would be reached in thirty to one hundred years, an estimate that was probably overly optimistic. We are witnessing the chemical pollution of the world.

We are also depleting and destroying the soil by over-harvesting, pollution, and inefficient use. Increased reliance on chemicals to hasten growth and enrich crops has unintended after-effects; erosion, floods, and drought further break down the fragile ecosystems of the poorest nations. Conservation as a worldwide movement has yet to prove effective. We have simply not yet shown enough restraint and concern to change the picture. Barry Commoner, the noted American botanist, has said, ". . . we are stealing from future generations, not just lumber and coal but the basic necessities of life: air, water and soil."

Production, manufacturing, and transportation all rely on fuels for energy. Electricity, air conditioning, and air travel consume incredible quantities of fossil fuels, which exist in finite deposits; some experts suggest that fossil fuel reserves will be gone in thirty to fifty years, yet these fuels seem necessary for the increasing standard of living most people want.

The "green revolution" and other efforts to increase world food output have been effective but are still no match for the widespread destruction of our natural resources. As much as ninety percent of the world's metals are used by one-third of the world's population. We are now beginning the incredibly complicated task of developing sound solutions.

Most tragic of all, each abuse against the environment affects every other part of the environment. Air, water, and soil are intimately interconnected. Polluted air affects water, soil, animals, fish, and human beings alike. Water carries pollutants directly to the earth, where they form a toxic bed further aggravated by pesticides and other chemicals. All wildlife is equally at risk, and species disappear at alarming rates. In our own time we have fundamentally disrupted the ecological harmony and balance of the planet. In our own time we have dangerously disrupted our natural process, and the bill is coming due. We have taken too much. Any hope for the future lies not in taking but in giving.

T·W·E·L·V·E

NATIONAL AND GLOBAL RESPONSE

America's Crisis

It was the best of times, it was the worst of times . . .
it was the season of light, it was the season of darkness,
it was the spring of hope, it was the winter of despair . . .

CHARLES DICKENS

The opening of *A Tale of Two Cities* is as descriptive of our age as it was of Dickens's. America keeps changing, and the new needs that accompany each change aren't always immediately mirrored by new giving patterns. New problems arise with a sudden urgency, and our response to them is limited. These problems are often confounding, bewildering, and frustrating because there are no simple solutions. Awesome forces are working against efforts to provide each of us with a life of dignity, respect, love, and equality such as:

- Economic downturns and financial insecurity.
- Reduction in government support of key social services.
- Inadequate housing for many of the nation's millions of poor.
- Increased crime and political corruption.
- Growing hostility and distrust and a lack of respect for life and property.

- A functionally illiterate population of some twenty million people.

- A staggering high-school dropout rate and bleak work prospects for dropouts.

- A sharp increase in homelessness, with no clear remedy for the problem.

- Continued growth of drug addiction and alcoholism.

- A substantial increase in America's aged population and the consequent severe strain on social and medical services.

- Runaway medical and health-care costs.

- Proliferation of the AIDS virus, with no cure in sight.

- High birthrate among the poor and underprivileged.

These are all urgent issues that need immediate attention. The private sector — foundations, corporations, and individuals — will need to provide greater assistance to nonprofit organizations struggling to relieve these social ills. We all need to become more personally involved, more generous. We need to become more responsive and sensitive to the needs of those less capable, less intelligent, less able to cope. This task will be difficult. There are substantial barriers to greater involvement, including:

- A decline of confidence in the abilities of the health and welfare services and a more survival-oriented attitude. A resurgence of the "look out for number one" syndrome.

- A steady decline in the influence of religion, the father of philanthropy. A recent Gallup poll showed that religion was considered "very important" by slightly more than one half (53 percent) of the population, a decline from a high of seventy-five percent in 1952.

- The negative impact of the televangelist scandals.
- The decline in the Catholic Church donor base, on a per-capita basis, to almost one half what it was twenty years ago.

American religious institutions are the nation's major nongovernment providers of human services. Many will be severely strained in the coming decade, especially facilities that provide medical care and health instruction; day care; free or low-cost meals for the elderly, indigent, and homeless; counseling; housing assistance; and care for the mentally ill or dying. Fortunately, religious contributions have shown a healthy increase in recent years. There is some room for hope.

Looking at the future, a recent blue-ribbon panel report from the American Council on Education cautioned, "The nation will suffer a lower standard of living, social conflict will intensify, our ability to maintain world market status may decline, our economy could falter, and our national security might be endangered." Individual concerns that also threaten the growth of community service and philanthropy include:

- Many Americans are showing signs of discouragement and frustration with increasing social problems. Will they increase their service efforts or begin a slow retreat to indifference? They wonder if they have become free labor — with no specific mandate.

- A sense of personal isolation, fragmentation, and alienation may be growing in America. Social conflict contributes to a divided and uneasy nation.

- People feel a creeping powerlessness, a lack of control over major issues such as illiteracy, substandard housing, drugs, crime, and homelessness. Despite the best efforts of individuals, institutions, and the government, these troubles continue to grow.

- The gulf between the affluent and the thirty-five million Americans who live in or near poverty keeps widening. This economic imbalance brings added stress to all of our social issues.

- Aside from church-related support, the average American only volunteers or contributes to one or two other charities or causes. This level of support is not sufficient to the tasks at hand.

- Fear, hostility, and distrust are beginning to diminish the empathy of dedicated and generous supporters. Many are unable to determine the legitimacy and effectiveness of both new and seasoned organizations. Corruption and scandal shake people's faith and willingness to help.

And finally, at the environmental level, there are a host of afflictions that beset America, including:

- Widespread air and water pollution.

- Deforestation, strip-mining, and overuse of public lands.

- Toxic waste, harmful pesticides, and inadequate waste management.

- Destruction of wildlife and the endangerment of species.

- Noise pollution, overcrowding, and allied environmental stresses.

There is much that is positive about America's response to social problems, but we certainly have our work cut out for us. These lists of woes, evils, and pressing imbalances are intended not to discourage us, but to dramatize our plight and our opportunities. As a nation we have overcome great environmental and social problems in the past: only a hundred years ago we had incredibly high infant mortality, uncontrollable epidemics, widespread child labor, gross discrimination by sex and color, outrageous exploitation of workers, unsafe drinking water, appalling sanitation, and severely limited educational opportunities. None of these evils has been eradicated, but all of them have been dramatically improved.

It is extraordinarily difficult to engineer effective social change. A single high-intensity assault upon a problem usually will not do the job; patience and determined effort by all, particularly individual initiative seem to produce the most enduring changes in the quality of life in America. It's all up to you and me, and since we have no direct control over each other, the responsibility for change and improvement falls on our own shoulders. When all is said and done, we hold the key to change and growth. We are the future.

The Global Ecological Disaster

We have developed a life style that is draining the earth,
without regard for the future of our children
and people around the world.

MARGARET MEAD

How is the world responding to the breakdown of our planet's ecology? Are we organizing to change our lives so that future generations will have a world as bountiful and as beautiful as the one we inherited? What are some of the factors that keep us from meeting this enormous challenge? Some scientists say it is already too late for our planet, that we have entered a "final countdown." The urgent needs of mankind for food, fuel, shelter, transportation, sheer survival, and of course some profits, have taken precedence over our care for the planet.

It is easy to be lulled into a false sense of security about the environment. The predicted catastrophes have not yet overtaken us: Global warming has not yet flooded the lowlands; there have been fewer authoritative reports about increases in cancer or the destruction of plant and animal life by ultraviolet rays than we might expect; every day it seems we hear of vast new oil reserves. For the most part pollution is an invisible enemy. And so industrial nations ignore environmental problems, trusting that the public will not be alarmed by what they cannot see or feel.

The problem is not so much that the public is indifferent or ignorant, but that government is slow-moving and that the need for profits sometimes coerces industry to behave in ways damaging to the environment. Most industries know how to use fuels and other resources more efficiently. They can switch to safer processes and sources, but profit margins are larger with the older systems already in place. Automobile manufacturers can already produce cars that use alternative fuels or less gasoline. There are safer, less dangerous pesticides. Many industries can easily diminish water pollution. We can restore the environment: forests can be replanted, erosion stopped, and seawater converted into fresh water.

However these changes will cost billions and will require great political courage. No multinational corporation willingly takes a drop in profits. No population willingly taxes itself. So we pass on our responsibilities to the next generation and rationalize our delay by saying that the negative effects on the environment are in dispute, that our existing social problems demand our full attention, and that the richer countries cannot afford to do more because of their own pressing problems. Do we use our resources to save a sick and starving child or to resurrect a withering coffee bush?

Even our most pressing problems — famine, war, AIDS — are not being well-handled. Most nations are poor in resources and in literacy, and debtor nations whose economic, political, and environmental systems are extremely fragile lack the ability to tackle even their own most significant problems, let alone global issues. In fact, most of the nations of the world have such distressing internal problems that they cannot even begin to lighten the burden of their suffering neighbors.

Survival and the development of an export economy are far more urgent issues for some developing nations than their own ravaged ecosystems. These nations justify the plunder of nature with the need to improve their tragic domestic situations. While they may be concerned about damage to the biosphere and global warming, about the survival of whales and buffalo, they have been forced to forego concern about most environmental issues simply to survive. When urged to try conservation measures, they are often coached by technologists from the very countries that depleted resources in the first place.

Most nations and peoples have no clear concept of stewardship of the earth. The disadvantaged nations are limited by their struggle for survival and self-sufficiency and, often, by the ignorance of their populations. The advanced nations know that the burden of change rests primarily on them, both to aid the poorer nations and to save the environment. But the burden is too great. Progress is made, but the population explosion, wars, pestilence, and environmental ills keep accelerating. Even strong nations can be overwhelmed.

Moreover, there is no credible blueprint for transformation of the environment. The simultaneous resolution of social problems and restoration of the ecological system seem beyond our capacity even to plan, let alone accomplish, and no real progress can be made until the public understands both the problem and its solutions. Until then, we will never agree to dismantle and replace much of the world's energy, transportation, and industrial structure, which is what it could take to transform the way we use land, fuel, and other natural resources.

Although we are beginning to cooperate internationally on critical issues like arms control, most nations are still primarily occupied with internal stresses. A study of well-educated and affluent Americans by the Overseas Development Council found that two out of three Americans think we need to solve our own social problems before we look to problems abroad. This attitude clearly limits our ability to act globally. In an inspiring speech, Manuel Arango, a noted world philanthropist and environmentalist from Mexico, sums up the message that we all need to enhance our global social and environmental awareness:

> In this way, the public and private sectors, in a relationship between politics and the market, seek to eliminate inequality and injustice by improving education, health, housing, security, the environment, and many other factors that lead to the desired quality of life.
>
> The unexpected and vigorous process of change and globalization is difficult to assimilate and more difficult to attain for many impoverished people in regions of the planet, who immigrate in search of opportunity or else hold on to the wealth of their cultures, finding in them the hope, wisdom, comfort, and spiritual strength that helps them to survive between the promises of an uncertain future and the realities of an unjust and pain-filled present.
>
> Democracy, free markets, and privatization are neither magical formulas nor static processes that can be reached easily and, once reached, can enable the population to rest in them and harvest the benefits. Experience has shown us that although these formulas are valid, they are perfectible and require, for their adaptation, the constant arbitration of the state or country.

Two Scenarios for the Year 2000

If you want to innovate, to change an enterprise or a society,
it takes people willing to do what's not expected.
Jean Riboud

The effort we make in the next few years to resolve our most pressing social ills will set the stage for the next century. As troubles multiply, each of us will need to volunteer, contribute, and advocate to bring about change. Even if we personally may have had little to do with the creation of these troubles, we are called upon nonetheless to help solve them.

As a nation we have drifted toward serious dysfunction for years. National and global problems have accelerated at a time when the government and the business community have been unable to marshal enough resources to significantly help. We have made progress in some areas, but in others our efforts have been about as effective as a Band-Aid on a gunshot wound. Every one of us will be needed if we are to reverse the deterioration all around us. The issues are broad in scope, and our responses need to be imaginative and all-encompassing. What we as individuals do — how we react and how we commit ourselves — is critical. Millions of people have been deeply committed and heavily involved for years, but if the problems are to be finally solved, it will take millions more of us in the future from all over the world.

I have constructed two possible scenarios for the results of our efforts as we bring closure to this century.

Scenario #1 — Into the Darkness

- Governments reduce funding for major programs and eliminate support for many small but deserving programs. Numerous environmental programs are dismantled and their funds used to prop up deteriorating health, housing, and education projects.

- An economic downturn forces many businesses to sharply reduce or eliminate their charitable contributions. Firms pull back from community support in response to profit-oriented managerial pressure.

- An economically depressed and financially anxious population reduces its contributions to religious institutions, forcing churches to curtail vital support services.

- Individualism and self-interest erode the effectiveness of nonprofit organizations as staff members struggle fiercely to save their own favorite program and their jobs. Leadership falters and effectiveness disintegrates.

- Organizational insecurity and chaos spill over into the volunteer ranks where frustration, confusion, and indifference are responses that destroy cooperation. The people who continue to serve form protective, fragmented groups that jealously guard their own turf.

- Volunteers and donors become disheartened and pull back from their commitments, which further reduces both manpower and the funds available for services. Budget battles escalate as professionals scramble for a specific place on the ark.

- The recipients of community services, poorly served, become increasingly resentful, suspicious, and uncooperative.

In this picture each setback feeds on the others, plunging the system of volunteer effort and spontaneous giving into chaos. As exaggerated as such a scenario may seem, it is possible. When the government pulls back and the economy falters, all of these conditions can arise. It's true that past recessions did not materially affect giving in America, but the need for services and problems with the environment are growing at a dizzying pace, while the economy, showing only modest growth, is not. There are indications that it will take years for the nation to overcome some of the financial excesses of the past decades.

Despite all governmental and economic predictions, the vitality of the nonprofit world and the effectiveness of service programs will be most influenced by what individuals do. It all filters down to the scope and intensity of my commitment to my neighbor and your commitment to yours. If we believe in the extended benefits of giving and volunteering and act on these beliefs, then we can avoid this first chaotic scenario.

Scenario #2 — Into the Light

Healthy and effectively functioning philanthropy in the future will require:

- An economy that is manageable and able to cope with financial stresses. Runaway inflation and collapse are avoided as enlightened cooperation out-paces greed.

- A long-term commitment to critical services and env-iron-mental programs on the part of the govern-ment. Rather than shift priorities at whim, the government steadily maintains funding and man-power for key programs.

- A population that has faith in the power and neces-sity of giving and volunteering, enough faith to will-ingly set aside at least five hours per week for community service and five percent of family income for charity.

- A citizenry that does not feel insecure or impover-ished when making large gifts.

- A society of individuals who can cooperate with their neighbors on a sustained basis for the public good.

- People who select volunteer assignments to maxi-mize their enjoyment of the process or experience.

- Religious teaching that focuses on brotherhood and is put into practice.

- An educational system that instructs and involves young people in community service. Service should be made part of the school curriculum to equip our young people to help disadvantaged neighbors.

- A government that uses public information and legislation to promote volunteer involvement. In education, government funding can be designed to establish more public service and nonprofit oppor-tunities.

Having described these two possibilities, it would be unfair to end this section without sharing some thoughts on how you personally might go about ensuring the second scenario. I can think of no person more qualified to help with this task than the psychiatrist and humanist M. Scott Peck. In his book *The Different Drum,* Dr. Peck eloquently describes the steps and actions we might consider: "The reality is that we are inevitably social creatures who desperately need each other, not merely for sustenance, not merely for company, but for any meaning to our lives whatsoever. These then are the seeds from which community can grow."

Peck endorses Alexis de Tocqueville, who in 1835 said the one characteristic that most impressed him about Americans was our individualism. De Tocqueville warned, however, that unless our individualism was balanced by other habits, it would lead to the fragmentation of American society and the social isolation of its citizens. To counterbalance that individualism, Peck urges us all to "Start communities. Start one in your church. Start one in your school. Start one in your neighborhood."

He goes on to quote the early Pilgrim leader John Winthrop, who described some of the major dimensions of "community": "We must delight in each other, make others' conditions our own, rejoice together, mourn together, labor and suffer together, always having before our eyes our community as members of the same body."

Finally Peck encourages us all, as he also does through the nonprofit group he founded, the Foundation for Community Encouragement:

> Start your own community. It won't be easy. You
> will be scared. You will often feel that you don't

know what you're doing. You will have a difficult time persuading people to join you. Many initially won't want to make the commitment, . . . Once you get started it will be frustrating. But hang in there. Push forward into emptiness. It will be painful . . . Don't stop halfway. It may seem like dying but push on. And then suddenly you will find yourself in the clean air of the mountaintop and you'll be laughing and crying and feeling more alive than you have in years, maybe more alive than you've ever been.

So start a community. Don't be afraid to fail . . . True community is always, among other things, an adventure, . . . and you will be able to share not only your fear but your talents and strengths. Out of the strength of your community you will be able to do things you never thought you were capable of.

These inspirational words offer both encouragement and direction. They could become a rallying cry as we lead ourselves into the light. That is my hope — I trust it will be yours as well.

T·H·I·R·T·E·E·N

VOLUNTEERS FOR THE PLANET

Communication Is the Key

Each time a man stands up for an ideal, or acts
to improve the lot of others, or strikes out against injustice,
he sends forth a tiny ripple of hope.
ROBERT F. KENNEDY

All relationships rely on communication. In business and in government, goals cannot be met without being properly defined through precise communication. Successful communication brings meaning and fosters understanding in any endeavor. Where communication isn't effective, it blunts opportunities for people to succeed in causes that are important to them.

Nowhere is good communication more important than in philanthropy and volunteering. Organizations that depend on donations and a corps of volunteers — nonprofit organizations — need even more sensitive and precise communication than do businesses. According to Dr. John Haggai, there is always the danger that "worthy thoughts were not given a chance because they were not presented worthily."

The role of communication in philanthropy is a complex one. Communication can be an appeal for financial support or a recruitment plea; it can be a description of services offered, goals to be achieved, or tasks to be accomplished. Some of the purposes of communication in philanthropy are:

- Promoting the benefits and rewards of giving and volunteering.

- Requesting funds, help, and advocacy in a spirit of sharing.

- Describing the needs and the mission of the organization.

- Matching people to challenging, satisfying assignments.

- Praising, acknowledging, and thanking donors and volunteers for their contributions.

- Campaigning to retain veteran volunteers and long-standing donors.

- Urging advocates to carry the message to legislators, government, and the public.

- Mounting special promotions to attract young people to community service.

- Lobbying for educational involvement in teaching about, encouraging, and sponsoring community service.

- Mounting campaigns to urge college graduates to choose community-service careers.

- Creating and promoting service opportunities that will challenge and reward students.

- Developing television programming that will teach elementary-school children the benefits of community service and altruism.

- Soliciting and listening to feedback from donors and volunteers.

- Publicizing and praising the efforts of volunteers in much the same way that Bush and Clinton have promoted the Thousand Points of Light program; establishing a databank of good deeds that the media can draw on, and encouraging them to do so.

- Conveying the organization's plans and problems to donors, volunteers, and staff.

- Holding brainstorming sessions to develop more effective and efficient programs, fund appeals, and advocacy strategies.

- Singling out energetic and active volunteers, donors, and advocates for special recognition and publicity.

- Selectively and efficiently setting forth the challenges and benefits of giving for prime donor prospects.

- Promoting the organization's programs to potential clients.

- Enlisting former clients in volunteer activities; soliciting advice, input, and feedback from clients.

Take a moment to review this list. Your cause or religious institution might benefit if you would undertake some of these communication tasks. There is plenty to communicate, and often staff personnel are too overworked to handle the job — perhaps you can help them or know someone else who can. Keep in mind that the most important communication of all is the tribute that you as a volunteer pay to the people who benefit from your program by showing up and sharing with them. By this all-important volunteer act on your part you tell them that they and the cause are valued.

Making a Difference Globally

It's not the difference between people that's the difficulty.
It's the indifference.
ANONYMOUS

The forces that drive nations are complex and shifting, and events and conditions seldom remain constant, so to suggest specific solutions to improve philanthropic activity around the world is a complex exercise and well beyond the scope of this book. Instead I would like to focus on what concerned Americans can do to meet the challenges of human need and ecological imbalance abroad, and to highlight some of the opportunities to make a difference we have here at home.

Take disaster and famine-relief programs, for instance. To help in these emergencies there are at least seven possible approaches:

- Donate money and resources to international relief organizations such as care, the Red Cross, unicef, the Interfaith Hunger Fund, Catholic Relief Services, Habitat for Humanity International, Joint Jewish Distribution Committee, Save the Children, Church World Service, and World Concern. I have served all of these agencies in one form or another as a fundraising consultant during the past thirty-two years and I can testify to their integrity and effectiveness. The Interfaith Hunger Fund, in fact, was born in my New York offices several years ago.

- Become involved in fundraising for one of these organizations. Become a volunteer or start your own grassroots solicitation of money, food, or clothing.

- Lobby the government to increase assistance to poorer countries. Help sway public opinion in favor of assistance. Write your congressmen and senators. Be an activist.

- Involve your friends in your project. Ask them to help you lobby and raise funds.

- Help local media inform the public about your cause.

- Think about specific ways to aid disadvantaged countries: one volunteer convinced a water-pump manufacturer to donate pumps and send technical advisors to a disaster area. You might canvass local manufacturers seeking gifts in-kind.

- Provide information to schools and youth groups. Become a spokesperson for your cause and enlist the support of concerned young people; numerous studies of young adults suggest that they are eager to volunteer if someone asks them and sets up a structure that makes it easy for them to become involved.

Many of these strategies can be used for other pressing issues, such as human-rights violations, the elimination of illiteracy, the rebuilding of a distressed ecosystem, or flood relief. The emphasis may shift to political action, lobbying and advocacy, or to the raising of funds for technical assistance, but the principles are much the same for any effort to generate support for international crises.

Though we may never visit a disadvantaged country or see the problems firsthand, we can still take steps to help people in some needy part of the world. Each of us has some capability: We can prepare press releases, assist at special events, enlist volunteers, lobby with legislators, appeal to corporations to become sponsors, or simply tell our friends about our concern and ask them to support it as well. All these efforts can help solve these global problems while bringing a new sense of joy and meaning to our lives.

Emergence of Global Responsibility

It seems obvious that before the end of the century we must accomplish basic changes in our relations with ourselves and with nature. If this is to be done, we must begin now.

M.I.T. Study of Critical
Environmental Problems

We live in a time of disaster with one crisis following another. As soon as we put out one fire, another more threatening one starts, and if nations are busy responding to the hottest flame, the most dangerous social evil, the most destructive war, they cannot take adequate measures to roll back the tide of social and ecological devastation.

Yet there are ways you can help the slow process of remedying global social and environmental imbalances. There will be no quick fixes; the problems are immense and deeply rooted, but each of us has resources that can be used to help create a more peaceful, secure, healthy planet. We sometimes feel powerless, confused, and overwhelmed, but we are not without talent and the capacity to bring about valuable changes.

First, you must realize that it is up to you as an individual to start healing the planet. The responsibility rests squarely on your shoulders and on mine. You don't need to make a grand gesture like selling all your property, donating the proceeds, and joining the Peace Corps, but you can take simple steps that can be enlarged upon by neighbors and fellow workers.

To begin with, you can learn more about environmental crises and suggested remedies. Read books on proposals to rescue the planet but be sure they are recent, as the field of environmental science changes constantly. Second, stop using environmentally dangerous products such as pesticides, plastics, and aerosol cans. As a consumer you have countless opportunities to vote against a company's policies of neglect — don't buy their products, or boycott indifferent manufacturers. Often the press will report on firms that are illegally dumping toxic waste and ruining the soil. Support legislation for greater monitoring and controls on pollution. Write your congressmen, educate your neighbors, write to the press, become a crusader against institutions that violate the environment. Advocate more stringent restrictions, more complete conservation, and the elimination of toxic manufacturing processes. Keep in mind that as you get into the battle to save the planet you will be going up against the forces of environmental exploitation. They are formidable foes and will resist any efforts to make them correct their excesses. The fight won't be easy.

Of course, you don't have to do battle alone. There are friends of the earth everywhere making their voices heard in state capitals, Congress, and throughout the world. Join with other concerned citizens who study environmental problems. Participate in rallies, demonstrations, and efforts to acquaint the voting public with local or national polluters. Encourage the governmental awareness of environmental excesses and pollution of the air and water. If you can, give to organizations involved in saving the environment.

Volunteer to work with them locally. Find opportunities to make a difference and jump in with both feet.

The world's social ills are daunting, but there is still much you can personally do to help. Start with a simple review of the needs that touch you most, the ones for which you have the most empathy. To some, local community issues will be most important; to others, national and international illiteracy and poverty may be uppermost. You may be one who tries to balance local activity with financial or advocacy assistance for international catastrophes or natural disasters. There are many more needs than we can ever possibly fill, which makes it important to help the causes you most believe in and that can give you a sense of satisfaction when progress is made. Move toward those that strike a responsive chord. Show your support by:

- Volunteering to serve the cause as a fundraiser.
- Making a contribution to your organization or lobbying and advocating for the cause.
- Giving food, property, or income to your organization.
- Volunteering your talents and services to help others in need throughout the world.

Certain causes may hold a special interest for you. You may decide to lobby, write letters, demonstrate, educate the public, or convey your views to local or national legislators. Do what Howard and Connie Clery did: work to have new legislation passed by Congress. Work to elect legislators who favor your stands on the social issues that most concern you. All of these ways of expressing your concern and compassion are likely to be available through your local church or religious institution. Join your talents and support to theirs, on behalf of the causes you care about.

In *No World Without End,* Katherine and Peter Montague issue this challenge: ". . . . across the land small groups of citizens have been and still are working in their various ways to provide a world of economic justice; clean air and water; uncontaminated soils; safe supplies of energy; safe, convenient, efficient, and low-cost public transportation; . . . clean, quiet, and safe streets; . . . thriving small-town and regional economies; adequate child-care facilities; inexpensive and humane health care; decent housing for all; easily accessible education services; widely available legal help; justice in the courts; clean workplaces, and meaningful work for all."

You can join them.

F·O·U·R·T·E·E·N

ACTING FOR THE FUTURE

Making a Difference

Where there is no vision, the people perish.
PROVERBS 29:18

The greatest barrier to improving society and the environment is indifference. So many people absorbed with their own needs and immediate problems do not see that all of us ultimately are affected when any one of us suffers. Children are sensitive to others around them, but as we grow older many of us become progressively more selfish. We don't lose our compassion and concern entirely, but often they are pushed aside by raw ambition, acquisitiveness, or sometimes the sheer need to survive in our demanding, pressurized society. If we are sufficiently troubled about the future, the resulting fear eventually breeds insensitivity. We lose perspective, to the point that all our energy and thoughts are for ourselves, not for others.

The same dynamic also operates in governments and nations. In a world of crises, fear and self-interest can be absolutely blinding. We try to deal with pressing issues through politics and organizations, through economic readjustment, self-sufficiency programs, and reforms, but while a government or its citizens concentrate on one crisis, three or four other crises grow in urgency. Revolution, reform, massive government aid, and the intense efforts of millions of dedicated people bring only limited or fleeting success.

The problems of the planet are far from resolved. Most grow more intense by the day, while the people who struggle with the degradation of the environment, human rights, famine, illiteracy, poverty, drug abuse, and homelessness grow weary and disillusioned. Others, who march to the drumbeat of self-serving contemporary values, don't see the meaning in philanthropic activities. Their indifference is profound.

We need to promote change if we are to emerge from the endless cycle of global conflicts and disasters. These changes cannot begin with governments, national leaders, or large multinational organizations; they must begin with you and me. John D. Rockefeller III put it very well in his book about philanthropy, *The Second American Revolution:* "The essence of private initiative is the decision by individuals to become involved and committed to something larger than themselves." And, as I've said, through consistent sharing and caring for something larger than ourselves we can become physically, emotionally, and spiritually whole. What an exciting possibility for each of us! We commit to changing the world and we get transformed for the better in the process.

To counter global catastrophes we need many resources and the most essential resource is committed and responsive individuals, individuals who will live by the concluding words of the Declaration of Independence: ". . . we mutually pledge to each other our lives, our fortunes, and our sacred honor." You and I are the most important resource in the struggle to save our planet. Change and growth can occur only when each of us accepts the truth that we must all give of ourselves so that we all may live. Transformation begins when we change our attitude and our actions. The effects of the fully committed few have only begun to stem the rising tide of social, political, and environmental problems. More and more of us must join them; more and more of us must learn how to give to live on this planet.

We have reached a stage where we cannot leave this work solely to institutions, governments, or leaders. In fact, we are living in a fool's paradise if we expect them to resolve our problems. When you hear over and over, "It's up to you; you are the only one who can do it, you are all mankind," your reaction may be, "I'm no miracle worker. The troubles in the community, nation, world, are just too enormous, too complex." Well, that's the point.

You are the miracle worker, and without your efforts there will be no miracle. At some level deep inside, you probably understand this. Naturally, you don't want to inherit the problems of the world, especially when you probably aren't directly guilty of anything more damaging than a little pollution. However, like it or not, the problems of the world are yours and will only get worse if you turn your back on them. You don't need another bundle of troubles, but that's the nature of social and environmental responsibility.

Each of us needs to accept a new mission. We cannot heal all of the problems of the earth by ourselves, but we have to believe that if enough of us commit ourselves and turn loose our energies and resources, collectively we can create wholeness. When an out-of-work rock musician, Bob Geldof, had the idea for musical support to aid hungry Africans, he couldn't foresee that his Band-Aid album and Live Aid concerts would net $83 million in relief funds — all he had was a vision and the commitment to act on it. You don't know how much of a contribution you can make until you start. You can energize yourself, go beyond your present limits, and just maybe change the world.

Once you decide you are ready to go the extra mile, you will need to reallocate your time, energy, and talents. More than one philosopher has said that the renewal of society and our planet must begin with a single individual — not the collective power of governments and organizations, but the responsible, committed, caring individual. Progress and change live only in the mind and the hearts of committed, compassionate citizens.

Perhaps you are trying to give some personal dimensions to this commitment. Given the resources you have, you might wonder how your efforts could have anything but the most limited impact. The truth is that you have many resources you may not be aware such as:

- Your energy and willingness to become involved.
- Your valuable time.
- Your talents, knowledge, and abilities.
- Your ideas and visions of a better world.
- Your compassion and concern for others.
- Your financial resources.
- Your commitment to use all of these elements to make a difference.

Given these essential building blocks, each of us can launch a program to begin changing conditions. The way to start is with baby steps, simple inquiries into whatever mission might best fit our talents and circumstances. Since many of us already volunteer, our commitment may simply mean greater involvement. None of this requires a grand entrance or great proclamations, just a deep, perhaps visceral recognition that we will need to invest a little extra effort, expend a few more hours a week, or give more generously.

Remember that any commitment you make is really with yourself; it can take whatever form you like but it needs to be freely made to be fully realized. Don't get involved just to please a relative or friend, though this may be the initial impetus. Once you accept the reality that a better world begins with you, relax in the knowledge that you will be the beneficiary of wonderfully rich, life-sustaining experiences. Your journey will not lead you down a road of sacrifice and drudgery. With grace and perseverance, you'll get much more than you give.

How to Begin: An Example

*Individuals . . . alone can make the decision to
become involved, and . . . if they do not, they miss their
most important chance to feel a sense of inner power,
to become whole human beings.*
JOHN D. ROCKEFELLER III

Once you have decided that you would like to take a stand for a better planet, you can begin tapping into a whole medley of resources. To look at some of them, let's return to the example of eliminating illiteracy in Cleveland, Ohio. Assume that this project vitally interests you.

Your first step is to discover how much illiteracy there is and what programs already exist to combat it. Start by contacting the government, social-services organizations, the Cleveland Board of Education, the United Way, and local foundations. Your aim is to educate yourself. You may have some well-formed ideas about illiteracy and how you would like to help, but you still need to get a briefing about the extent of the issue and what is already being done to correct it; the more information you have, the better the chances are that you can help.

Once you see the big picture, you may see a role for yourself. You may, for example, discover that there is a well-organized and comprehensive program for young children and high-school dropouts, but no programs for illiterates in the workplace, whether American adults with no schooling or people whose native language is not English. At this point you may feel enthusiastic about a project to help illiterate adult Americans. What you need now is support, guidance, funding, teachers, pupils, classrooms, and promotion; perhaps you also need city approval of classroom materials. You make up a list of what you think you need. Then, once you've gotten by the sinking feeling that what you are trying to do is impossible, get in touch with people who might help you. These might include:

EDUCATION EXPERTS
- Cleveland Board of Education
- State Board of Education
- U.S. Department of Health, Education, and Welfare
- Local teachers' union or council
- Retired teachers' association

From this group you are seeking guidance, contacts, potential teachers, used books, and suggested curricula.

GOVERNMENT LEADERS

- Cleveland social-services directors
- Mayor's office
- Housing, transportation offices
- State officials, senators, representatives
- Federal officers, congressmen, senators

These can provide program funding, classrooms, books, supplies, even information about which business establishments may have illiterate workers.

FUNDING SOURCES

- Local United Way
- Local and regional foundations interested in education
- Local universities and private schools
- Church groups
- Government grants
- Local businesses, large and small
- Concerned citizens, friends, neighbors

Once you have done some planning and enlisted others in the project, you need a budget. It should estimate the cost of classroom rental, books, supplies, a central information office, phones, publicity, and transportation. You can build a volunteer teaching staff and use empty classrooms at night or on the weekend.

The Business Community

- Large and small manufacturers
- Service organizations
- Business groups, such as the Better Business Bureau
- Labor unions

Virtually every local firm is a potential source of financial support and of people in need of education. In large organizations you can get in touch with the human resources manager or Employee Assistance Program for contributions and publicity. Greater literacy will benefit industry as well as individuals, so don't be shy about asking businesses for help — shake their "Money Tree."

The Media

- Local daily and weekly newspapers
- Local television and radio stations
- Local or regional magazines
- Business and social-service newsletters

The media can be a valuable partner in your efforts, publicizing your program and class schedules, but make sure you tailor your publicity to the people you are trying to reach. In this case your prime audience is not able to easily read written materials, so you need to gear your publicity to their literate relatives, friends, and co-workers who'll be able to carry the message for you. You should use every source available to you at little or no cost: bear in mind that your advertisements may qualify as public service announcements. The media can help you raise funds by doing human-interest stories about your efforts, and don't forget local editions of multicultural media such as Hispanic newspapers.

VOLUNTEER TEACHING STAFF

- Local colleges and universities (faculty and students)
- Public schoolteachers
- Retired or former schoolteachers
- Retired professional people
- Active professional people
- Church group members

You may find that recruiting a teaching staff is easier than attracting pupils; for many there is a sense of shame about illiteracy. To some extent, your printed invitation may need to be directed at concerned family members and acquaintances, urging them to inform illiterate friends and relatives.

Whatever cause or organization you choose, remember that there are many resources that can be enlisted and cultivated in your efforts to bring about change. Using them effectively requires ingenuity and perseverance, and don't underestimate the desire of others to help when they see something good happening. Programs that are accomplishing something have a way of attracting support from the most improbable sources. To expand your role you have to become a "town crier," publicizing the cause of literacy whenever and wherever you can. Become a walking conversation about your project. Enlist everyone you can.

You'll be amazed at how many resources become available once you go into action.

The Global Horizon

*If we are to lift ourselves out of this morass, we must
shift our sights from the superficial to the sacrificial.*
JESSE JACKSON

Our global focus has become clouded and our vision
obscured. We have not done a very good job of understanding other human beings. As long as our concern includes
only our own race, country, community, religion, or family
we will continue to live in a turbulent world. In the past,
war and revolution have been the principal means of resolving conflict, but once we see that there is a possibility of
living happily and safely together on the earth, we can start
building a new unified world.

Nationalism, ethnic and religious prejudice, and closed
or exclusive affiliations divide us. Under their influence we
can hate, violate human rights, punish others economically, even go to war and feel good about it. Despite international forums like the United Nations, we still are not
always able to reason together peaceably.

There are some elements in our society trying to teach
nations to restrain themselves; for instance, most religions urge us to mediate disputes rather than take up
arms against each other. However, nationalistic spirit
largely dictates global policy, and nationalist fervor is
sometimes fanned by religious leaders who misinterpret
the teachings of their community. Discrimination occurs
at all levels. Some nations become more self-enclosing
and protective. A universal or global mind-set is emerging, but there are dozens of nations and millions of
nationalistic citizens who prefer to dwell upon differences rather than focus on similarities and cooperative

opportunities. Much of this has to do with economic and political power. Degradation of ecosystems, pollution, and exploitation of the poor are too often by-products of the efforts of multinational corporations to extend their markets, increase production, or promote consumption of toxic products.

Human beings create governments to keep themselves safe, but often, in attempts to maintain an ideology or preserve a lifestyle, these governments can oppress or disenfranchise millions. In many parts of the world human life has little sanctity or value, a reality that is unlikely to change much in the near future unless we shift our focus. For centuries nations have proclaimed the sanctity of the individual citizen and then enslaved, banished, or exploited them. Oppression, economic greed, corruption, suppression of human rights, and plundering of the environment are, unfortunately, the norm in our global society.

I don't know any grand solutions to the complex and ever-expanding array of global disturbances. I do know that we need to change our focus. For too long national governments have been the central players in global deterioration. In the interest of security, economic advancement, and cultural and ethnic survival, we have given governments great powers. As a result, the individual has abandoned or relinquished much personal power. In many nations, individual power has been taken away by dictatorial governments with disastrous results.

Most governments function ineffectively, while some function destructively. We have all seen the proliferation in various countries of government programs that favor the rich, the powerful, and the warlike. If the billions spent for defense by the nations of the world were redirected to social programs, hunger, disease, poverty and illiteracy would most likely end. As a nation and as a member of the global community, our own country has the resources to transform our hungry, impoverished, troubled world.

Since World War II we as a nation have chosen to expend great resources on war and communist to thwart encroachment in the name of "protecting our way of life." Protection it may have been, but at what cost? We might have established an adequate protection for perhaps one half of the billions we allocated to defense. We saw Vietnam as an enormous threat and we overreacted — instead of using our resources to improve life and heal the planet, we spent hundreds of billions to wreak havoc and destruction . . . and we divided our own nation. Understand, I am not against military action, though I am against wars of aggression as a means of resolving problems. While I was working on the manuscript for the second edition of this book, America, along with an international coalition, interceded in Bosnia, and I believe that our decision to do so, when months of negotiation were to no avail, was just and right.

Now that the conflict is over and the coalition has won, we have a unique opportunity to show our commitment to environmental issues. We can even do it as our troops remain there. I like the idea Edwin Dillard, a seventy-seven-year-old retiree in Greenville, Tennessee, expressed in a letter about another conflict (even though other methods were finally used):

> Experts said it would take months, perhaps years, to drive Saddam Hussein out of Kuwait in a ground war. Now they're saying it could take several years to put out the oil wells burning across the

country he was actually driven out of in a little less than four days.

Why not turn the troops and equipment and ingenuity already over there against the massive oil spill and devastating well fires Hussein has unleashed on the world? Couldn't the bombers that are already there be loaded with high explosives (or cement, or sand) and sent against the fires? I don't know whether such an effort would be practicable or if it would work in the end, but I think it's important to try anyway. We need to show we care as much about the environment as we do about containing aggression. We need to find our sense of proportion.

We certainly haven't found this proportion in the past. The issue that disturbs me most about the huge military budget is that it virtually ensures that no meaningful progress will be made in the war on poverty, inadequate health care, illiteracy, crime, drug addiction, and the other social ills that beset us. I'm convinced that we have had the focus on the wrong set of issues. There has to be a more responsible way than war to resolve nationalistic disputes and acts of naked aggression. These issues are exceedingly complex and provoke intense feelings, and I don't see many short-term solutions on the horizon.

I want to suggest, though, that a way to start is to plan. I propose a major planning effort, at both the national level to reorder our domestic priorities, and at the international level to deal with the monumental problems of disadvantaged nations and global environmental threats. If we are to survive and progress, we need to alter our priorities drastically or we will surely see even greater domestic unrest, human suffering, and environmental collapse. We cannot forever postpone or hastily patch the cracks in the dam. These are my suggestions. I hope they are worth promoting:

- We should review and prioritize all the major social and environmental issues at the national and international level.

- We should give the highest priority to the preservation of life, protection of health, provision of shelter, and protection of human rights. All nations starting with our own must hold these as inalienable rights.

- We must be willing to support the programs that have been given priority. Once elective bodies have established priorities, we need to act in concert to implement them. Our government raises funds in order to execute programs as we, the people, direct.

- We need to learn everything we can about the extent of our social and environmental ills and the cost of correcting them. With this knowledge we can petition others and the government to develop and fund needed programs. This requires public education to inform us all about the severity of our social and environmental troubles and what each one of us can do to help overcome them. Americans can move from entrenched self-interest to massive self-help and support.

- Power needs to be rooted at the level of the individual. We need to understand that we already have adequate resources to destroy the roots of poverty. During the Depression and World War II, we were a nation in crisis and we triumphed. We can do it again.

We can harness both the powers of our government and our own personal powers.

- To establish sensible social programs that the whole nation will endorse, we need to be willing to endure adjustments and sacrifices. We might, for example, consider a more progressive distribution of wealth tied to work effort and taxes. At present, according to IRS data, the top income quintile (twenty percent) in America earns on average almost eight times as much as our poorest quintile. In Japan the ratio is five to one, and their economy hasn't suffered. I resist thinking in terms of wealth redistribution, but it's an alternative always worth considering.

- The number of people giving and serving and the number of hours expended both need to increase. The nonprofit sector will need to reallocate priorities and rechannel resources, but it must remain innovative and experimental, developing new and better programs: It should not simply fill in the holes missed by the big-government paving machine.

- Our best economists, environmentalists, philanthropists, and government leaders should join experts from all over the world to prioritize issues and pledge resources. The economically advanced nations should play a significant financial role in renewing the social and economic structures of disadvantaged nations. These nations cannot, with present resources, overcome their problems. Advanced nations must be prepared to provide emergency aid and resources to move disadvantaged nations to a state of self-sufficiency.

A New World Leadership

The sole meaning of life is to serve humanity.
LEO TOLSTOY

What kinds of leaders can help the world move forward through all its manifold social and environmental problems? I believe we need a shift in the paradigms of leadership. Instead of pursuing power and gain for nations and for themselves, leaders need to seek solutions to the great crises of the world.

The world has too little enlightened leadership, and too many leaders are nationalistic in their approach to global problems. This is lamentable, but I don't think that too much blame need be attached to it; after all, politics and statesmanship exist to protect, expand, and promote the economic and political aims of individual countries. Leaders to a large extent merely reflect the motives of the populace. I can't recall any warlike, aggressive nation ever electing a pacifist leader. The basic motives that guide an advanced nation are economic and personal gain. In less advanced countries, benevolence and cooperation are often displaced by naked aggression and the desire for power, control, and private use of relief money.

Leadership frequently amounts to the unbridled practice of greed for personal gain. Desire for power and raw ambition are more often the prerequisites to leadership than compassion and humility. The noted world religious leader Dr. John Haggai, in his book *Lead On* writes, "Love as a characteristic of leadership seems to be out of place, yet there cannot be true leadership without love. The love of which I speak . . . is the outgoing of the totality of one's being to another in beneficence and help." The mind of the politician is inscrutable, and leadership is often a reward for long-time service in the ranks of a political party, and politics rarely rewards humanitarian impulses.

Of course, not all world and national leaders are venal. Their dilemma is that they have a constituency to serve; their task is to satisfy the needs of those who put them in power. They are often forced to make decisions that penalize, disenfranchise, or limit support for their nation's most impoverished and troubled people. Sometimes they are pressured to make decisions that go against common respect for human rights and compassionate concern. Private interests and a desire for power are usually close to the throne. Anyone who has been a student of leadership knows that leaders are subject to all sorts of frailties — I beg your indulgence for repeating this observation.

I find it extraordinarily difficult to believe that a leader who commits his nation to a war of aggression can also have a deep compassion for his nation's illiterate disadvantaged. It's hard to understand how war can be beneficial to any populace or environment, for a war machine drains funds that could be employed to resolve social ills. Yet supremacy and dominance are the goals of many nations, and many of the world's leaders achieved their positions by aligning themselves with the powerful, the ambitious, and the driven. Such leaders are not the most sensitive, compassionate clan on the face of the earth.

Today more than ever we need leaders who can plan and manage the process of healing our wounded planet. Establishing sensible, reasonable goals and prioritizing the problems to be faced call for the talents of the most skilled and humane individuals, not those wedded to seats of power or rigid ideologies. The new leadership will need great sensitivity and the ability to gain cooperation from the uncaring and unwilling. This leadership must some-how balance the need for economic progress and national security amid political and social turbulence. The task of reconstruction will be most demanding.

If this mission is to be successful, it cannot be left in the hands of those who favor power and self-gain. We need to empower experts in the arts of sacrifice, mediation, com-passion, perseverance, persuasiveness, and planning. In trying to restructure many of the world's most fragile and troubled economies, these new leaders will have to do battle with the entrenched and protective interests of the world; they will be downsizing or dismantling many war machines; and most critical of all, they will be asking nations to set aside sovereign rule and cooperate with poli-cies that may run counter to their immediate interests.

Such leaders will need diplomacy, tact, perseverance, and deftness. Their tasks will require the perspective and vision of world planners, not the insular restrictive myopia of chauvinistic politicians or governmental bureaucrats. These leaders will also need to harness gov-ernmental efforts to accomplish the tasks of environ-mental reconstruction.

How can any body of humane, intelligent, and qualified leaders adequately evaluate the world's tragedies and mis-eries, assign priorities, and prescribe remedies? Nations have found few remedies to social ills and even fewer to environmental problems. History is filled with conflict, strife, and war, but very few humane cooperative ventures. The United Nations and its predecessor, the League of Nations, were to be forums to facilitate peace, but their track records have been less than inspiring. Somehow nations must be convinced that global cooperation ant planning are the only sane courses of action.

Time is running out. There must be an unequivocal commitment by each nation to devote much of its resources and manpower to the restoration of global balance and the correction of internal ills. So far, fragmented programs, world conflict, and war have defeated our early efforts in numerous embattled nations. Some programs, like the Marshall Plan at the end of World War II, have worked and worked well; as we did then, so today we have the resources to end our social and environmental troubles, but first we must overcome economic and political interests, the quick-fix mentality, and crippling nationalism and aggression. Early progress will likely spring from educational efforts. World leaders and the public at large must be made fully aware of the disastrous state of the world and the economic, political, and social excesses that have led us to this global crisis.

Who can we turn to for such an assignment? The answer is: everyone. All nations need to inform their citizens of the nature and extent of our problems. Government leaders must extract concessions from their citizens to permit cooperation on a world basis. They also need to commit some of their resources to global reconstruction; if only a few nations agree to such a course of action, the renewal effort won't work, because the problems are too extensive. Many nations will need to commit to two broad agendas:

- To pledge some of their resources and manpower to assist other nations and help reverse world environmental imbalances.

- To pledge a significant proportion of national resources and manpower to correct and eliminate internal social and environmental ills. For some of the poorest nations, this will require aid and technical assistance coming from abroad.

Willingness to cooperate and a firm commitment by each government to follow the reconstruction plan will be essential building blocks in any renewal effort.

New Leaders

To begin this gigantic effort, I propose a global task force of philanthropists, economists, business leaders, governmental experts, statesmen, environmentalists, scientists, medical experts, and sociologists. This umbrella task force would assess the current and future impact of each social and environmental problem at both the national and international levels. It would assign priorities and design relief and renewal programs in cooperation with national governments. Implementation of the plans would have to be borne by individual countries using their own resources or international aid. The task force should also evaluate each nation's resources and abilities to contribute to other, less fortunate nations. Implicit in this global approach is a relinquishing of some national control, a commitment of resources, and a willingness to plan and execute in an ecumenical spirit.

There is risk and uncertainty in any plan this size, of course, and the success of this global program will depend upon the reactions and commitments of the superpower nations and the wisdom of their leaders. Success will involve a significant redistribution of the world's wealth and resources and quite a bit of sacrifice, but disease, famine, poverty, and faltering ecosystems will not diminish on their own. Misery will expand and grow unless we band together in one universal effort.

In America, we must evaluate our potential leaders in terms of their sensitivity to the needs of the disadvantaged. In the past we have not always selected the most humane leaders. We need to be clear about the role we want our elected representatives to play, for they control taxation and the national budget. As individuals, we collectively have the power to shift priorities and resources. We can, if we choose, contain those who trash the environment or allocate huge sums to the military. We can use our energies to advocate, lobby, vote, inform, rally, educate, and support the causes we believe in.

Who will finally lead us into global recovery? My answer is . . . *you*, a person who has discovered the life-enhancing benefits of daily practice of the Golden Rule. *You*, a person who gives to live and in so doing changes the lives of others much as you change your own.

F·I·F·T·E·E·N

TREADING THE GIVING PATH

You Can Become a Giver

There is nothing new about the Giving Path. Literally millions of people through the ages have understood intuitively that the way to their own health, happiness, and peace of mind lies in helping others. Giving and sharing have always been the way wise men and women have built the world, for others and for themselves. What is new is our understanding of how philanthropy affects our bodies and minds. The extraordinary findings of the last two decades of research enable us to say with assurance what we always suspected was true: to give is to live.

When we give our time, our money, our talent, our concern, and our compassion for others to a cause, we receive more than we give. Our hearts, our immune systems, and our general health all improve. Our minds are clearer and more focused, we have a better and more positive picture of ourselves, and we are better able to sort out and meet the competing demands of our lives. We feel better about ourselves, we know we are loved, and we can love all the more in return. We change for the better when we help other people, and at the same time we change their lives and the world.

There are ways to become involved in giving and sharing which help us get the greatest return physically, mentally, and emotionally from our investment of time and treasure. The first thing we need to remember is that *our lives are important.* What we value is important, and therefore we can choose causes to make the best use of what we have to offer. Our time is important, and so there are ways to incorporate sharing into our daily routine. We can do what we set out to do if we are honest about what we want and feel and if we plan to make the best use of what we have.

The Giving Path is also a path to family renewal. We can begin by sharing what we have and then enlisting our wives or husbands, children, even parents and brothers and sisters in our causes. Children learn to lead wholesome and generous lives by being encouraged to follow the Giving Path early in life; young people are brought to a greater respect for others and themselves by helping and sharing. We learn how we can make the greatest possible use of what God has given us in this life so that our values can continue to shape the world after we are gone.

When we walk the Giving Path, we release tremendous power in our own lives. The power we may have looked for by heaping up wealth or manipulating others we can find when we help others. Our lives begin to blossom when we follow the spiritual principle of "doing unto others as we would have them do unto us," and we experience a powerful integration of the different forces in our lives as we redirect much of our drives for power and control into the work of sharing and giving.

In praising, acknowledging, and recognizing others we discover that we unleash their energies for good and create powerful human networks that can accomplish tremendous things. A generous response to others enables us to see that they are indeed "points of light," giving us, our children, and our friends models of what we might do ourselves. Sharing our troubles with others in like circumstances helps us learn from one another and points a way out of the despair that our addictions and afflictions can lead us into.

When we begin to help others, our hearts will grow and our minds will inevitably awaken to the tremendous needs of people around the world and to the degradation of our planet's environment. The Giving Path helps us become aware of terrible realities yet at the same time empowers us to improve our society and the world. The growing problems in America and abroad compel each of us to try to find solutions,.and when situations call for changes in political and economic structures, as they surely will, we will find that the generosity of heart we learned on the Giving Path will give us the strength and courage to face the changes with equanimity and grace.

Giving to live is in fact the only way to live fully. When each of us shares what has been given to us, we gain a new life; if each of us hangs onto what we have, it will never seem enough. Even the richest people in the world think they have to have more if they do not have the habit of sharing what they have. They are letting what they have determine who they are.

The loving energy of a person like Mother Teresa, a Catholic, Princess Diana, a Protestant, or Victor Frankel, a Jew, could transform the world, even if he or she doesn't possess a dime. What they did have is the indomitable human spirit given by their Creator, and so they were endowed with almost limitless potential. You possess that same spirit. When you walk the Giving Path — when you give to live — your spirit will expand, your powers will grow, and you will be able to bring about great changes and transformations.

The material gifts we are given never seem enough until we have shared them with others. When we give to a

264 • MORE GIVE TO LIVE

good cause, we are linked with others in the solidarity of giving but also in the solidarity of human need, because every human being needs something. When we are in solidarity with each other, we learn what our real needs are. Our lives become more focused, and we value the good things we have earned or been given all the more because we see what they have been able to accomplish. Our lives are simplified and our spirits strengthened when we give. Sharing puts us back in touch with each other.

Most of all, walking the Giving Path connects us to the great Giver himself. We know that it is God's nature to give and give without measure or complaint, even when His gift and His love are ignored or abused. His overflowing love is what makes the world and our own lives possible, so when we feed a hungry man, when we help a child learn to read, when we help fund a clinic, when we give clothing to the poor, we are connecting ourselves to the love of God. We are increasing and multiplying the giving energy of the divine in the world. We are helping bring about the Kingdom of Heaven on earth.

Giving is living. Without the gift of life from our parents, we would not exist; without their nurture when we were infants, without help from society as we went to school and grew in stature and knowledge, without the help of others (often strangers to us) as our careers and lives unfold, we would have no life. Everything we are and everything we have is a gift. What little we have earned can never be enough to pay back the entire gift given us — we are called to invest in each other. Giving is living because in giving our lives are made better in every conceivable way. When we give to others, when we share our time, talent, and treasure, we do not end up with less in our accounts, but more.

So I call on you to begin a life of giving. Walk the Giving Path. Share what you have with others. Let your light shine. Give as you have been given to, and more will be given to you, in greater measure, pressed down, and overflowing. Join the Giver and all his human helpers through the ages. Your life will never be the same.

BIBLIOGRAPHY

ALLEN, Derek. A Comparative Study of the Tax Treatment of Donors to Charity in Various Countries. Tonbridge, Kent, England: Charities Aid Foundation, 1987.

"Altruism's Own Rewards." Foundation News. (Washington D.C.) (May–June 1988): 29ff.

"A Time to Seek," Newsweek, 17 December 1990.

AUTRY, James A. Love and Profit. New York: William Morrow, 1991.

"A Windfall Nears in Inheritances from the Richest Generation." New York Times, July 22, 1990, p. 4.

BELLAH, Robert. Habits of the Heart. Berkeley: University of California Press, 1985.

BENSON, Herbert. The Mind/Body Effect. New York: Simon & Schuster, 1979.

———. The Relaxation Response. Boston: G. K. Hall, 1976.

BLANCHARD, Kenneth, and Spencer Johnson. The One-Minute Manager. New York: William Morrow, 1982.

"Breaking a Spring Tradition," USA Today, March 15, 1991, p. D-1.

BREMNER, Robert H. American Philanthropy. Chicago: University of Chicago Press, 1988.

BUCKLEY, William F. Gratitude: Reflections on What We Owe Our Country. New York: Random House, 1992.

BUFORD, Bob. Half Time. Grand Rapids, Mich.: Zondervan Publishing House, 1994.

Burns, David D. *Feeling Good: The New Mood Therapy*. New York: William Morrow, 1980.

Buscaglia, Leo D. *Loving Each Other*. New York: Holt, Rinehart and Winston, 1984.

Canfield, Jack, et al. *Chicken Soup for the Soul*. Boynton Beach Fl: Health Communications, Boynton Beach, Florida, 1997.

Carlson, Martin. *Why People Give*. New York: Council Press, 1985.

Carlson, Richard. *Don't Sweat the Small Stuff*. New York: Hyperion, 1997.

Castro, Janice. *The Simple Life, Time*, April 8, 1991, pp. 58–63.

Chambre, Susan Maizel. *Good Deeds in Old Age*. Lexington, Mass.: Lexington Books, 1987.

"Charitable Giving and Philanthropy Soared from 1987 to 1989." *The Chronicle of Philanthropy* (Washington, D.C.), October 16, 1990.

Charitable Giving: What Contributors Want to Know. New York: National Charities Information Bureau, 1988.

Cohen, Lilly, and Dennis Young, eds. *Careers for Dreamers and Doers: A Guide to Management Careers in the Non-Profit Sector*. New York: Foundation Center, 1989.

Cornuelle, Richard. *Healing America*. New York: G. P. Putnam, 1983.

————. *Reclaiming the American Dream*. New York: Random House, 1965.

Cousins, Norman. *Anatomy of an Illness*. Boston: G. K. Hall, 1979.

————. *Head First: The Biology of Hope*. New York: Dutton, 1989.

Csikszentmihalyi, Mihaly. *Flow: The Psychology of Optimal Experience*. New York: Harper & Row, 1990.

Daring Goals for a Caring Society: A Blueprint for Substantial Growth in Giving and Volunteering in America. Washington D.C.: Independent Sector, 1986.

DASS, Ram and Paul Gorman, *How Can I Help? Stories and Reflections on Service.* New York: Alfred A. Knopf, 1985.

DE TOCQUEVILLE, Alexis. *Democracy in America.* New York: Viking, 1956.

DOUGLAS, James. *Why Charity? The Case for the Third Sector.* Beverly Hills Calif.: Sage Publications, 1983.

DROTNING, Philip. *Putting the Fun in Fund-Raising.* New York: Contemporary Books, 1979.

DUNN, Thomas. *How to Shake the New Money Tree.* New York: Viking Penguin, Inc., 1988.

DYE, Thomas R. *Who's Running America?* Englewood Cliffs, N.J.: Prentice-Hall, 1990.

EMRIKA, Padus. *The Complete Guide to Your Emotions and Your Health.* Emmaus, Penn.: Rodale Press, 1986.

ERIKSON, Eric H. *Childhood and Society.* New York: W. W. Norton, 1950. *Identity and Life Cycle.* New York: W. W. Norton, 1980.

FRANKEL, Victor. *Man's Search for Meaning.* New York: Washington Square, 1963.

FRANTZREB, Arthur C. *Not on This Board You Don't.* Chicago, Ill.: Home Books, 1997.

————. *Philanthropy is Both Giving and Receiving.* Fund Raising Management, January, 1984.

Gallup Organization. *Religion in America.* Report 259. Princeton, NJ: Gallup Organization, 1987.

Gallup Survey. *Non-Profit Times.* November 1988,2(8), p. 1.

GAYLIN, William. *Caring.* New York: Alfred Knopf, 1983.

Giving and Volunteering in the United States. Washington, D.C.: Independent Sector, 1988.

Giving USA: The Annual Report on Philanthropy for the Year 1997. New York: AAFRC Trust for Philanthropy, 1998.

GORDON, Sol, and Harold Brecher. *Life Is Uncertain, Eat Dessert First!* New York: Delacorte Press, 1990.

Greene, Robert, and Oprah Winfrey. *Making the Connection.* New York: Hyperion, 1997.

Haggai, John. *Lead On.* Waco Tex: Word Books, 1986.

Handlin, Oscar, and Mary Handlin. *The Wealth of the American People: A History of American Affluence.* New York: McGraw-Hill, 1975.

The Health Benefits of Helping. Washington, D.C.: Spring Research Forum, Independent Sector, 1989.

Hodgkinson, Virginia. *Dimensions of the Independent Sector: A Statistical Profile.* Washington, D.C.: Independent Sector, 1984, 1986.

————. *Dimensions of the Independent Sector: A Statistical Profile.* New York: Foundation Center, 1990.

Hodgkinson, Virginia, and Robert Wuthnow. *Faith and Philanthropy in America.* San Francisco: Jossey-Bass, 1990.

Hurley, Dan. "Getting Health from Helping," *Psychology Today,* (Jan. 1988).

Jaffe, Dennis. *From Burnout to Balance.* New York: McGraw Hill, 1984.

————. *Healing from Within.* New York: Alfred Knopf, 1980.

James, Estelle. *The Non-Profit Sector in International Perspective.* New Haven, Conn.: Institution for Social and Policy Studies, 1980.

Jampolsky, Gerald. *Out of Darkness into the Light: A Journey of Inner Healing.* New York: Bantam Books, 1989.

Joseph, James. *The Charitable Impulse.* Washington, D.C.: Council on Foundations, 1989.

"Learning to Give." *USAir Magazine,* (Dec. 1990): 42ff.

Lawson, Douglas M.. *Volunteering: 101 Ways You Can Improve the World and Your Life.* Poway, Calif.: ALTI Publishing, 1998.

Lewin, David. *Community Involvement, Employee Morale and Business Performance: A Study of U.S. Companies.* New York: Working Papers, 1991.

Luks, Allan. "Helper's High," *Psychology Today*, (Oct. 1988): 38ff.

—————. *The Healing Power of Doing Good*. New York: Fawcett/ Columbine, 1991.

Lynch, James. *The Broken Heart: The Medical Consequences of Loneliness*. New York: Basic, 1979.

Magat, Richard. *Old Wine or Potent Brew*. Unpublished, 1989.

—————. ed. *Philanthropic Giving: Studies in Varieties and Goals* (Yale Studies on Nonprofit Organizations). New York: Oxford University Press, 1989.

Marts, Arnaud. *The Generosity of Americans*. Englewood Cliffs, N.J.: Prentice Hall, Inc., 1966.

—————. *Philanthropy's Role in Civilization*. New York: Harper & Row, 1953.

Maslow, Abraham. *Religious Values and Peak Experiences*. New York: Viking, 1970.

Materazzo, Joseph: *Behavioral Health*. New York: John Wiley and Sons, 1984.

May, Rollo. *Man's Search for Himself*. New York: W. W. Norton., 1953.

Measurable Growth in Giving and Volunteering. Washington, D.C.: Independent Sector, 1985.

Millar, Bruce. "Baby Boomers Give Generously to Their Charities, Survey Finds, But Their Willingness to Do Volunteer Work Is Questioned," *The Chronicle of Philanthropy*, July 24, 1990.

Montague, Peter, and Katherine Montague. *No World Without End*. New York: G. P. Putnam's Sons, 1976.

Nichols, Judith. *Changing Demographics: Fund-Raising in the 1990's*. Chicago: Pluribus Press, 1990.

Norman, Michale. "Volunteers in Dual Roles on Campus," *New York Times*, February 10, 1988.

O'Connell, Brian. *America's Voluntary Spirit*. New York: Foundation Center, 1983.

————. *Philanthropy in Action.* New York: Foundation Center, 1987.

————. *Volunteers in Action.* New York: Foundation Center, 1990.

ODENDAHL, Teresa. *Charity Begins at Home: Generosity and Self-Interest Among the Philanthropic Elite.* New York: Basic Books, 1990.

O'NEILL, Michael. *The Third America: The Emergence of the Non-profit in the United States.* San Francisco: Jossey-Bass, 1989.

ORNISH, Dean. *A Program for Reversing Heart Disease.* New York: Random House, 1990.

————. *Love and Survival.* New York: Harper Collins, 1998.

————. "The Healing Power of Love," *Prevention Magazine,* (Feb. 1991): pp 60f.

ORNSTEIN, Robert and Sobel, David. *The Healing Brain.* New York: Simon & Schuster, 1987.

————. *Healthy Pleasures.* Reading Mass.: Addison-Wesley Publishing, 1989.

OSTROWER, Francie. *Why the Wealthy Give.* Princeton, N.J.: Princeton University Press: 1995.

PANAS, Jerold. *Born to Raise: What Makes a Great Fundraiser, What Makes a Fundraiser Great.* Chicago: Pluribus Press, 1988.

————. *Excel.* Chicago: Pluribus Press, 1998.

————. *Megagifts.* Chicago: Pluribus Press, 1984.

————. *Official Fundraising Almanac.* Chicago: Pluribus Press, 1989.

PARE, Terrence. "Passing on the Family Business," *Fortune,* (May 1990) p: 81 f.

PAYTON, Robert. *Philanthropy: Voluntary Action for the Public Good.* New York: Macmillan, 1988.

PEALE, Norman Vincent. *How to Make Positive Imaging Work for You.* Old Tappan, N.J.: Fleming Revell Co., 1982.

————. *Power of the Plus Factor.* Old Tappan, N.J.: Fleming Revell Co., 1987.

PECK, M. Scott. *The Different Drum.* New York: Simon & Schuster, 1980.

————. *The Road Less Traveled.* New York: Simon & Schuster, 1987.

"Private Students Volunteer: The Privileged Aid the Poor." *New York Times,* April 4, 1991, p. A-16.

"Pro-Social Behavior," *Psychology Today,* (Oct. 1988): 34ff.

ROCKEFELLER, John D. 3rd. *The Second American Revolution.* New York: Harper & Row, 1973.

ROGERS, Carl. *On Becoming a Person.* Boston: Houghton-Mifflin Company, 1961.

ROSSO, Henry, et al. *Achieving Excellence in Fundraising.* San Francisco, Jossey-Bass, 1981.

ROWE, John W. and Robert L. Kahn. *Successful Aging.* New York: Pantheon Books, 1998.

SACKS, Oliver. *Awakenings.* New York: Harper Collins, 1973.

SCHULLER, Robert. *The Be-Happy Attitudes.* Waco, Tex.: Word Books, 1985.

SELYE, Hans. *The Stress of Life.* New York: McGraw-Hill, 1976.

————. *Stress Without Distress.* Philadelphia: Lippincott, 1974.

Seven Steps to Happiness. *Psychology Today,* (July/Aug. 1989): 37ff.

SHEEHY, Gail. *Passages: Predictable Crises of Adult Life.* New York: E. P. Dutton, 1976.

SIEGEL, Bernie S. *Love, Medicine and Miracles.* New York: Harper & Row, 1986.

SIMON, Sidney B. *Getting Unstuck.* New York: Warner Books, 1988.

————. *Values Clarification.* New York: Hart Publishing, 1972.

STANLEY, Thomas, Williams Danko, *The Millionaire Next Door.* New York: Longstreet Publishing, 1997.

STOKES, Bruce. *Helping Ourselves: Local Solutions to Global Problems.* New York: W. W. Norton 1981.

"The ABC's of Philanthropy: First Lesson Is Well-Learned," *New York Times,* March 15, 1991, p. A-16.

"The New York Times Neediest Cases," *New York Times,* December 17, 1990.

SYME, Leonard. "People Need People." *American Health,* (July–Aug. 1992).

U.S. Department of Education, "Youth Indicators 1988"

VAILLANT, George. *Adaptation to Life.* Boston: Little, Brown, 1977.

VAN TIL, John, et al. *Critical Issues in American Philanthropy.* New York: AAFRC Trust for Philanthropy, 1990.

————. *Mapping the Third Sector: Voluntarism in a Changing Social Economy.* New York: Foundation Center, 1988.

Volunteering and Giving Among American Teenagers 14 to 17 Years of Age. Washington, D.C.: Independent Sector, 1990.

WARSCHAW, Tessa. *Rich Is Better.* New York: Doubleday & Company, 1985.

WEISBROD, B.A. *The Non-Profit Economy.* Cambridge Massachusetts A: Harvard University Press, 1988.

What Americans Think: Highlights. New York: Overseas Development Council, 1987.

WILLIAMS, Redford. *The Trusting Heart.* New York: Random House, 1989.

WILSON, Marlene. *You Can Make A Difference!* Boulder, CO: Volunteer Management, 1990.

WOLPERT, Julian, et al. *Key Indicators of Generosity in Communities: The Failure of the Non-Profit Sector.* San Francisco: Jossey-Bass, 1992.

A World in Need: Opportunities and Changing Roles for Philanthropy. Kent, England:Interphil, 1983.

WUTHNOW, Robert, and Virginia Hodgkinson. *Faith and Philanthropy in America.* Washington, D.C.: Independent Sector, 1990.

YANKELOVICH, Skelly, and White. *The Charitable Behavior of Americans: A National Survey.* New York: Rockefeller Brothers Fund, 1986.

ABOUT THE AUTHOR

Dr. Douglas M. Lawson is the author of the award-winning bestseller *Give to Live: How Giving Can Change Your Life* (ALTI Publishing, 1991), currently in its sixth printing and in three foreign-language editions (Spanish, Italian, and German), *More Give To Live: How Giving Can Change Your Life* (ALTI Publishing, 1998), and *Give to Live: A Stewardship and Development Program for Your Church* (Abington Press, 1995). He is also the author of *Volunteering: 101 Ways You Can Improve the World and Your Life* (ALTI Publishing, 1998). He has written numerous articles for such national publications as *Fund Raising Management, U.S. Air, Southern Bride,* and *Servant Leadership.* He has been the publisher of a monthly newsletter, *Philanthropic Trends Digest,* AS WELL AS eight editions of *The Foundation 500.* Dr.

Lawson has produced numerous audiotapes and video-tapes, including *The Artful Asker, Give to Live,* and *A Basic Fundraiser Course.*

Dr. Lawson holds three academic degrees: a B.A. from Randolph Macon College, a B.D. from Drew University, and a Ph.D. from Duke University. He is a member of three honorary fraternities: Phi Beta Kappa, Omicron Delta Kappa and Pi Gamma Mu. He is a member of the board of directors of Fleetwood Enterprises, a New York Stock Exchange corporation, and he is on the advisory board of the Yale Divinity School, the board of the Houston Junior Achievement, and the American Leprosy Mission board. He has served as a member of the Charitable Giving Task Force of the Million Dollar Round Table and the Board of the Joffrey Ballet.

In his professional life, Dr. Lawson serves as the founding chairman of Douglas M. Lawson Associates, Inc., a fundraising and management consultant firm which, to date, has served more than one thousand clients throughout the world and assisted clients in raising more than $2 billion. Dr. Lawson is a frequent speaker and lecturer throughout the United States, Mexico, and Canada.

Douglas M. Lawson Associates, Inc. has represented such clients as chapters of the American Red Cross, Habitat for Humanity International, Special Olympics International, Junior Achievement, CARE, United States Committee for UNICEF, Girl Scouts of America, Texas Tech University, Rhodes College, and the Robert Schuller Ministries.

For more information on the services of Douglas M. Lawson Associates, Inc., or the availability of Dr. Lawson for speaking engagements, please contact us any time, twenty-four hours a day:

Dr. Douglas M. Lawson
Douglas M. Lawson Associates, Inc.
545 Madison Avenue
New York, NY 10022

Voice: 800/238-0004
Fax: 212/759-1893
E-mail: doug@douglawson.com
Home page: www.douglawson.com

TO BENEFIT SOCIETY

ALTI Publishing specializes in tailor-made books that support the missions of nonprofit organizations. We are seeking additional book concepts which will help improve the human condition and assist worthy causes.

If you have an idea for a great book, we would like to speak with you. The project may be in manuscript form, merely an idea, or somewhere in between. The topic may be either linked directly to the mission of a specific nonprofit organization or a general subject with broad application.

Special editions of all our existing books are available with your logo, name, and personalized greeting included.

ALTI Publishing
P.O. Box 28025
San Diego, CA 92198
Phone: (800) 284-8537
FAX: (619) 485-9878
Email: whilbig@altipublishing.com

Call for Quantity Discounts